FROM SEOUL TO SOUL

A Mother's Journey, A Daughter's Dream

CHINA ROBINSON

Photos are from China Robinson's personal family collection
Photos of Chanel Iman are from her personal work portfolio
Vogue Korea cover - photographer Oh Joong Seok

Published by China Robinson
CR Words Published & Company
Literary Consultant – Patrick Oliver – SpeakLoudly.com
Editor – Melissa L. Moore
Interior Book Design by Relana Johnson – DigiVixen Graphics
Cover Design by Tyora "Ty" Moody – Tywebbin Creations LLC
Bio Photo by William Looper
Photo of China with Chanel – William Looper
Advisement/1st draft edit and sub title creator – Nicolas Boggs

CRwordsPublished.com
China@CRwordsPublished.com

Library of Congress Catalog in Publication on file.
Memoir
ISBN 978-0-9896082-1-3

Dedication

To God be all the glory!

I dedicate this book in loving memory of my Father, Reverend Ewing A. Robinson (1915–1979), and my Mother, Mrs. Shirley Irma Dean Robinson (1915–1982), whom I cherish in my heart forever.

I also dedicate this book to my amazing children and granddaughters:

Kemarah Kim (Asia), Chino Christin, Chanel Iman, Sanai Alon and Dylan Michelle

You are my everything. I give to you my story in order for you to know the struggles that made me the mother and grandmother I take pride in being. Also, much love to my Son-In-Law, Sheldon "Tony" Guillory.

I love you with all of my heart — pinched tight, from one side of my finger all around the world to the other side of my finger, and nothing can get in between (you know what I'm talking about).

Acknowledgements

I truly thank ALL my family and friends for their constant encouragement throughout the many times I've talked about writing this book. There are so many of you that I can't begin to mention you by name; although, I know you know what part you contributed. With family and friends by your side and God leading the way, all things are possible. Thank you!

Special thanks to Patrick Oliver for walking me through the many perils of this author's quest to complete my book. You are an incredible friend and literary consultant, whom I treasure. Your support, unique gift and expertise in getting things done are truly awesome assets. I value you with the utmost respect!

Melissa Moore, as my gifted editor, your work is amazing. You have inspired me to take hold of the confidence I needed to release my work to the world. I thank you for your valuable uplift in sharing my voice!

Thanks to Tyora Moore and Relana Johnson

for the creative cover, layout and design of this book. What an amazing job!

Kim and Margot, thank you for sharing your stories with me and allowing me to share them with the world.

Vivienne (Candy) Crenshaw, I have so much to say about your hands-on support in the completion of this book. So, feeling blessed, I will only say this in caps: THANK YOU SO MUCH!!! XOXOXO

Each one of my children and grandchildren are my biggest supporters. I love and thank each one of you. Kemarah, your strength is incredible. Thank you for letting me share your personal ordeal. I am proud of your accomplishments. Chanel, I add this to you, because through your dream to be a model, you gave me a glorious ending to my story that I've wanted to write for so long. For that I will always be grateful. Thank you.

Last but not least, thank you to World Vision, the Holt family and Holt International Children's Services for your work and efforts in saving the thousands of ostracized children of Seoul, Korea. The many "war babies" would not have had a chance at life without your love. May God bless you always and forever.

CONTENTS

Foreword

When I think of my own childhood and how full of love and commitment my family was in embracing any and all of my dreams, I truly can appreciate the journey my mother traveled from a childhood that began in despair to a woman of faith, love, and character that I look up to and admire. Throughout her lifetime, the stories of her struggle have lifted me, knowing the strength it took to overcome the negative forces she faced on the way to becoming the backbone I depended on as a child. Even now as an adult, I welcome her wisdom and truly am honored to be her daughter.

I stand tall, not only because of my height, but certainly because Mom has taught me to hold my head high and love the skin I wear. She inspires me every day, knowing the fight she was once up against, challenged with prejudice and cruelty, finally gave way to self-acceptance that led to a more positive and amazing life.

In this story that she so openly shares with the world, my courageous mother reaches out to a vast scope of readers, some of whom perhaps are going through or have gone through experiences and challenges similar to the ones she so fearlessly overcame. She reveals her own life lessons, free of the fear of judgment, with the prayer that what she gathered from her journey will help others come to a better understanding of what victories are up ahead for them.

There's no doubt in my mind, having grown up knowing and seeing in action Mom's giving, nurturing, and unbreakable spirit, the pages you are about to read will touch your heart in some way. This compelling story transforms insecurities into power of owning one's own dignity, freeing paths one is destined to travel. Mom has taught me, "No matter what your beginnings are, it's up to you to take your roots and nurture them until they grow strong and powerful."

I have trusted my mother's advice and guidance throughout my life and career as a model. She has mentored me into becoming a positive and strong woman. My success is attributed to her faith, beliefs and support, and she has taught me to always be myself and never let anyone shatter my dreams. Because of my mother's influence, I realize that I am the "power of one" that keeps those dreams alive.

This book is subtitled, *A Mother's Journey, A Daughter's Dream*. In the pages, our legacy unfolds. Even though the title fits well, I hope the reader knows that the story is not limited only to my mother's journey, or only to my dream. It is really about many journeys and many dreams—those of my sister, brothers, and nieces, and those of other extended family members and friends. I thank mother for having the courage, wisdom, and above all a great love for people, to share this story that will encourage so many. I love you, Mom.

Chanel Iman

Preface

From Seoul to Soul

This is the story of my life. It takes you from my kindergarten years to becoming the mother of a supermodel who helps me go full circle in embracing my roots. Between these events, I had to find my way to a place of peace, understanding, and empowerment.

From the time I was a small child until well into my adulthood, I felt the uneasy feeling of not belonging and struggled through my own insecurities of being an African American woman with Asian features. But when I went on a journey to find a little lost girl born in Seoul, Korea during a time of cruelty and despair, I discovered I had to rejoice in what I was blessed to have. My life wasn't so bad after all. As I relived a past that nearly destroyed my path to true happiness, I realized I had allowed decades of bad situations to capture me and take away my ability to save myself. I fought to gain back the power to free me and control my own destiny.

Over fifty years as history took a complete transformation I learned many lessons about myself and the world as I once saw it and the world as I see it today. The many hurts and heartaches brought me to a realization that I too had to transform and find my own soul. In this book, I share with you these lessons, hurts, and heartaches and bring you with me on my journey of discovery and self-awareness.

In my search to find the little girl that was ostracized from the lingering effects of the aftermath of the Korean War in the '50s, I discovered the world I was having a hard time being accepted in was far more receptive than I wanted to admit. For years, I almost allowed one person to use my insecurities against me and take away my power to control my destiny. From abuse to victory, my journey to find the little lost girl rescued me. I discovered an inner strength that helped me find a way to reclaim the power I needed to lead and direct my own path.

I grew up during an era when prejudice was covert and socially acceptable. This was true not only for the larger, wider community of Americans, but also for the marginalized, insular, often self-segregated neighborhoods in which Mexican Americans, Italian Americans, African Americans, and Asian Americans lived. Social settings were often rife with confusion and racial tension. In my own social circles, I encountered people who could be bitterly judgmental, especially about skin color, casting a person out merely because his face was darker, lighter or just different than theirs. These harsh judgments gave way to challenges no one should ever have to go through. As I have had one revelation after another on my journey to recovering me, I realized that many of those people who were so quick to judge me on my skin color or the shape of my eyes just didn't know any better. That is not to say they didn't cause any damage. Their ignorance set the tone for my own self doubt, which I had to overcome by accepting me. Once I did, a whole new world evolved and I soon found myself returning to the very ones who rejected me fifty years earlier. They now welcomed me with open arms through an amazing celebration that put my daughter on the cover of *Korean Vogue* as a black beauty. The very black skin that took me from Seoul to Soul and bridged the gap to my divided worlds was connecting me to people who had for so long rejected me. Finally they recognized me as one of their own.

Introduction

When there is a war, children suffer the most. The aftermath is full of casualties and orphans with nowhere to call home. We are surrounded by thousands that need our help, but few are reaching out to help them. For those who do, heartless bureaucrats and red tape get in their way, making it almost impossible to give a helping hand or a vision of hope.

How many times do you turn the channel when you see child hunger and bad conditions in other countries, or even in your own back yard? How many times do you close your eyes at the disgusting sights of how horrible things are, because you feel it is too large for you to undertake or cope with; or it will just take too much of your time to reach out yourself? Has guilt pushed you to the point you almost do something, then you let it pass?

There are those who do make the effort, who do reach out and follow through, who do save lives. They have a calling. It doesn't have to be you. But it could be...

We have to stop striving for what is useless, and apply our efforts to sustaining the betterment of useful goals for ourselves and all people. Giving is essential to survival. Superficial fascination is a waste of developmental time. It robs you of that inner power to feel what's real; instead of a solid base in which to enhance your mind and heart, or to help you build character in completing your soul.

One should not be weighed by the color of their skin, the size of their features, where they are from or even where they have been, but by the size of their heart. I have traveled many roads during my lifetime—some leading me on a path where I found meaning and value; others taking me off course where I was lost. However, with that being said, I have learned that on every road there is a learning tree from which to gather fruit. After I have taken what I need to learn of this fruit, I try to plant its seed so it can continue on and live for someone else who is hungry. The fruits I have gathered on the roads of my life's journey have given me nourishment to fill my starving soul. I am now full, my vision is clearer, and I find myself traveling down a road that carries me safely home every time I wonder: Who am I? Where am I? How did I get here? Who have I helped along the way? Have I accomplished my purpose in life? These are questions we all should continuously ask ourselves. Whatever answers we come up with truly reveal who each of us really is.

It took many years for me to heal and finally wake up each day accepting myself as being whole. It took a lot of time for me to come to terms with being the blessed person that I am and understand that God does work in mysterious ways. He does love all the little children. "Red and yellow, black and white, they are precious in His sight." He had purposely brought me from Seoul to soul.

CHAPTER 1

The Power of One

I learned very late in life the importance of self-empowerment and the ability to love your own existence in whatever arena you are graciously blessed to be in. There was once a time that it took me fully falling out of sync with who I thought I was, claimed I was, and who I had been working so hard at proving I was, to realize I didn't even know myself at all.

My challenges were wasted on needless signs of approval or achieving acceptance by people who basically were cruel. I felt bitterly exposed to eyes that were always on me, judging to keep me in my place—wherever they felt I should be. I went to great lengths to conceal my hurt and to prove I was an exact ditto image of them.

As I grew up in the ghettoes of Los Angeles, in a predominantly black neighborhood, what was hard to take was rejection from those to whom I belonged. My people, my own community. After all, I was raised to believe in them. To take pride in

1

their accomplishments and to strive to be like their best and help those of them that were less fortunate. They were my people. But I grew up struggling with "Am I theirs?"

But as the world turns and better days rise up, I've come to a different place in life. A place of comfort, confidence, and joy. I find myself now and again wondering why I wasted so much time on such nonsense and frivolous strife. I've come face to face with myself, discovered I really like me a lot regardless of what others might see. Mind you, my picture of me is quite different than that of others. Most people attempt to set me apart because of the color of my skin, the size of my eyes, or the texture of my hair. Their disavowing criticism castigates or compartmentalizes me because of these characteristics. I often want to say to these people, Are you kidding? They'd have to be not to realize that these features are my attributes, not my faults. Their harsh judgment is not just ignorant, it is also tasteless.

I wasn't always able to so easily dismiss this kind of trivial behavior. I can do it now because my journey has led me to the self-aware, confident woman in control of her own sense of self I was born to be. A delayed peace, strengthened by an enlightening journey to find myself, courageously embraces who I am and the discovery of my true roots. A peace that runs deep in my soul and binds me to the pride of just being me. With this I have chosen who I want to be: a self-assured being that has taken back the power to design my own path. At last I have overcome my fears of not fitting in. I've victoriously grown to realize I no longer worry about how others feel. I no longer need the approval of others. Why did I ever?

The answer is simply this. Like most kids that try to "fit in," no matter what I did, I was never happy being different. We never seem to be accepted as being the same, which we so much want or need to be. At least that was how I felt for most of my young life. Yet anyone and everyone who has achieved greatness and been successful in this life is a bit different or unique. They have to be. If not so, they would not have stood out or been special enough to make an impact on their lives and the lives of others. People that are just like everyone else blend into the sheer ordinariness of life and mostly go unnoticed. I must have been out sick the day that lesson was taught. I lacked an understanding of that theory in my young life, ultimately compromising a healthy beginning.

My struggle began as far back as I can remember, September 1960. I was four just short of turning five. I had spent that entire summer eager for the fall to come so I could start kindergarten at Compton Avenue Elementary School right in the heart of Watts. This was before the ever so famous riots. It was a time of peace and unity, when many inner-city blacks were finding their place of service in the community through socialism. An upward bound effort to heighten the awareness of black pride and Black Power! A coming-together generation of Soul Sisters and Brothers. Nat King Cole and Ray Charles had laid the grounds for a new generation and a new Motown rising to the top with a young group of stars who would make music history and eventually become legends. Aretha Franklin, Boy Wonder (Stevie that is), The Supremes, Marvin Gaye and endless "Do Wop" groups.

My parents and I had shopped for new school clothes at the Sears and Roebuck in downtown Los Angeles, one of the biggest stores in Los Angeles at the time. We'd gone to The ABC Market, a chain of grocery stores once known to the LA area, to get my school supplies and some last minute things at Hudson Department Store in the neighborhood. After shopping the three stores, I ended up with: four outfits, new underwear, bobby and knee-high socks, school shoes, a cute little lunch pail, a pad of paper with wide green writing lines and ribbons for my hair. I was now ready and complete with everything I needed. At least I thought so. Everything except the tools to handle the struggle I would have to endure the rest of my life.

It's my first day of kindergarten. The air was filled with a scent that only comes around once a year somehow dividing the summer smells from the alluring back to school aromas of new clothes, books, supplies, and a host of classmates to share your long days with. Mom and I entered the schoolyard that day with the morning dew still brushing across our faces as we passed rows of bungalows full of classrooms for the upper grades. I had no idea that when we got to the far end of the school where two connecting classrooms were fenced in to keep the big kids out and the kindergarteners in, I would by the end of the day feel the afternoon heat sweating me like I was cornered in a cage. Up until that day, whenever we drove past the school, I'd proudly point to the two little rooms on the corner lot of the school with its own private yard of swings, monkey bars and black tarred asphalt, reminding my mother that's where I was going to go one day. I just couldn't wait. But that anticipation turned into disappointment.

Sitting on one of two round, spiral-woven rugs— one for the girls, the other for the boys—in my brand new classroom, I squirmed with excitement. I was a real schoolgirl. I looked up at my new teacher smiling down on us, calling out the roster to make sure all of her little darlings had arrived on the first day of school. In alphabetical order, one by one, the teacher called out our names and placed little name tags strung with thick colorful yarn around our necks. I was one of the last few to be called, my last name being Robinson. But finally, I got to have one of those bright handcrafted name tags. They looked as if she had spent all summer making them. I proudly stood up as my new teacher put the name tag over my head. Beaming, not really looking and still at a clumsy age, I attempted to sit back down on the round carpet. My attempt was off centered, however, and I almost sat on another little girl by accident. It was at that moment that the short life I'd known as being like everyone else ended.

I looked wide-eyed into the face of the little brown-skinned girl I'd nearly pinned to the carpet. Before I could get out an apology, she cut her eyes at me crossly and slightly shoved me aside.

"Get off me!" She yelled in a snooty squeal that somehow defined her as the boss of things.

She continued, pointing a tiny finger towards another part of the round carpet.

"You sit over there with her because you have no eyes and she has no lips. You guys look funny."

Then she took her index fingers and pulled her eyes straight out to each side while sucking in her lips in an attempt to caricature what she saw as flaws in my face and the face of the other unfortunate girl she had called out.

Everyone laughed and started making the same faces. Why were they laughing? I looked at Yvonne, the girl she was calling "no lips." Yvonne looked back at me. Neither of us cracked a smile. The joke was on us, but we just didn't get it. My mother had promised me I'd make new friends and that school would be so much fun. This wasn't fun and it certainly wasn't funny. The teacher was busy calling the last names on her list and giving out tags, so the little girl's hurtful antics and the class making fun of Yvonne and me went unnoticed a while longer than it should have.

When it at last dawned on the teacher that the class was being disruptive, she loudly tapped her thick wooden ruler on the desk beside her and gently warned us to be quiet. That was the first rule of the classroom that we learned. Whenever we heard her make that unnerving sound, it meant everyone had to be quiet and whoever didn't obey would have to sit on the red zone rug in the corner of the room, alone and secluded. I heard someone whisper, "That's where they should sit."

I didn't speak up and accepted the humiliation. I found myself slowly scooting over next to the girl with no lips. We sat there, Indian style, looking at each other, wondering if we could go home to our mommies. At least that's how I felt. I couldn't wait to tell my mother how wrong she was about school. She had convinced me since I had on my new pink skirt and matching blouse with the pretty pearl buttons in front, white lace ankle socks I had begged to wear with my new black leather Mary Janes, it would be the best day ever. She had carefully picked through the ribbons and found just the right one for my long puffy pony-tails that were perfectly twisted and held together with matching barrettes clasping the tip ends. Mother was so proud and told me, "Everyone is going to love you. You look very cute and pretty. Yes, they'll love you." No they didn't!!!

For about a month after that, "no lip" Yvonne and "no eyes" me kind of depended on each other. But that didn't last very long. It turned out, as time went on, Yvonne finally won the class over because that little mouth of hers sure could make some noise and talk a lot. As I can recall, she became the leader of her own pack, of which I was not a member. Instead, quiet me never went a day without constantly being reminded I had no eyes. Slant Eyes. Tight Eyes. "Ching Chong China" was my name. Other kids who were not in my class straight out called me a "Jap."

Kids would run up to me on the playground and try to mimic the Chinese language while asking me if I understood them. Embarrassed and demoralized, I cried often. When I told my mother, bless her, no way did her heart understand, she'd always told me to ignore bad kids and know that I am beautiful. But mother wasn't there taking the teasing and having to stand up to any of them. She was not the one running away from their teasing or playing alone because the other kids said if anyone played with me, they would catch my "yuckies" and would end up with tight eyes also. "Sticks and stones will break your bones, but words will never hurt you," she'd quote. Mother was wrong. I was so hurt. Cast out and having few friends in grade school, I'd turn to my father and tell him how hurt I was. Being the minister he was he'd place his big hand on my head, say his "heal her in the name of Jesus" prayer, and tell me something like, "What a friend we have in Jesus."

I remember all these details from my first year of school as if it were yesterday. It was so traumatic for me, profoundly impacting my ability to be myself from that first day of kindergarten forward. No one had ever made me feel enormously small, ugly, or so far out of place. I felt trapped like a sparrow with a broken wing. I wished the teacher had sent that girl to the red zone all by herself the very first time she'd said those demeaning words. Who knows? The words might not have ended up becoming so powerful. I don't remember what that girl's name was, the one who started it all, but I vividly remember she wore a blue dress. I now look back and think "Devil in a Blue Dress." That would have been the perfect name for her. If only I'd had the courage to speak up or do something in my defense that first day of kindergarten, maybe things would have turned out different for me. But there it was. The start of a sore that wouldn't heal.

By the third grade buying friendships had become a habit. Somehow I always had money to buy candy from the candy man around the corner from the school. My mother would walk me to school most of the way, but she allowed me to walk the last block alone. While she watched me hurry along the last few steps, I'd wave a final good bye. Then the minute I saw her heading home, I'd turn the corner, sneaking back around to go into the candy store and buy a box of goodies to give to my classmates. It got so bad, at one point, when I didn't have any money saved in my little bank, I became desperate.

It is true that desperate situations call for desperate measures. Shamefully, I began to steal money from my aging grandmother's purse. She was very old and never knew how much money she had. Going to school with a box of favorite candy to give away (selectively) was always my moment to shine. I'm talking the store's box that they sold one piece at a time out of. The stock box. The whole caboodle. Everyone liked me when they were devouring the sugary candy, convincing me they were my best friends. That is, until the candy was all gone and I'd end up at the end of the day still trying to fit in. That'll teach me. Right!

It must have been about the third or fourth grade when I passionately begged my cousin Candy to come and go to school with me for a year. Her real name is Vivienne, but we called her Candy then (we still do). It must have been because she was sweet, with a milk chocolate brown complexion coloring her heart shaped face. I just knew it would be great to have a home-grown companion to take to school and be my very own friend. Her mom, Auntie Johnnie, agreed and allowed this union to take place.

So, sometime during the first quarter of the next school year—it may have been fourth or fifth grade—my cousin Candy and I walked into school as schoolmates. It didn't matter that she was not in my class, we were natural allies. Oh my...we were so excited. We would take on the name-calling, bullying cliques at Compton Avenue Elementary School together! But when Candy got there, she instantly made friends. Lots of them. It wasn't hard to figure out why. On that heart shaped face were the most beautiful big round eyes that had the longest eyelashes you've ever seen. That milk chocolate brown skin was perfect and was stretched out over a long, tall, and thin body. Nothing like my pale light skin and definitely not my tight eyes. Plus, I was short and somewhat stocky....What was I thinking?

The only thing Candy and I had in common was our long puffy braids we wore alike to match our look-alike dresses. Funny. Away from school, everyone always said we looked like twins. But now, here at this school, everyone I said that to said I was a liar. They didn't even believe we were cousins. I became even more of a joke. So, the only way I could ease my pain for inviting Candy to come to my school, was to treat her badly. And that I did. I treated her so badly that one day my mom announced Candy was going back to her old school. That had to be the most unfair thing I had ever done to anyone. I'm not sure if I ever apologized to her. I think at some point I must have because today we are so close, but for the record...

Candy I am so sorry!!! I know she has forgiven me because today she is one of my best friends and is still like a sister to me.

Finally the day came when my name changed from "Ching Chong China" to "Kung Fu" Terror. My one and only memory of anyone liking me in grade school was a chubby boy named Anthony. We were in fifth grade when he asked me for my phone number and said he wanted me to hear a new song by The Jackson Five (I think it was "ABC"). So I gave him my number and told him if my parents answered to tell them he wanted to ask about homework. He called and I listened to the song, knowing I was not allowed to play R&B, pop or any type of music at home other than gospel.

My father was a Baptist minister and we just didn't have anything but gospel music to listen to. In fact, by now, I was the pianist at my father's church (I'll tell you about that later). Anyway, after Anthony let me hear the Michael Jackson song, I played him something from our collection of gospel albums I thought was upbeat. I can't remember what, but it was all I knew or had for that matter.

The next day at school, he apparently had told his boys about our phone call, saying I called him.

They gave him a hard time about liking the Ching Chong China girl. He denied it and started teasing me about the gospel music. I was embarrassed yet again. Out of frustration, I called him a "fat pig." I knew better. Perturbed by my attack on his physique, his mini crush subsided, and my short-lived friend decided he was going to kick my ass after school. That was all there was to it.

When school was out that day, I don't know where it came from, but I had had enough!!! I stood up to him on that playground after school, with a big crowd egging us on and watching what I'm sure they thought was going to be his triumph when it was all over. God must have been watching, too, and was definitely on my side because Anthony picked the fight right in front of a bench. Now, that bench was between me and my opponent, so when he took a swing at my head giving it all he had, which would have been a mighty blow, I saw it coming. I ducked down, almost tilting my head into his guts. Then somehow, miraculously, he lost his footing and flipped over my back.

Laughter shocked my ears as I found my chest rising to victory. From that day on the kids stopped calling me Tight Eye Ching Chong China and started telling everyone I knew Kung Fu. They dared anyone

14

to mess with me, because I could flip or karate chop anyone if they teased me or pissed me off.

The constant teasing eventually subsided and my last year at Compton Avenue Elementary School was memorably calm. With my confidence on the rise, I managed to graduate as one of the class, even making some friends that didn't mind hanging with me. I went on to junior high and high school without any more slights about or reference to my tight eyes. The only thing that kind of lingered from my painful adolescence came after my parents enrolled me in Faith Lutheran private school. A yellow bus came to pick me up on the corner each day. In my neighborhood, at the time, any yellow buses that showed up usually were for mentally retarded or handicapped kids (today we call them challenged). So, you know, the kids on my block had to make sense of seeing me get on that yellow bus and that's when a few mean spirited kids started saying I was retarded.

Just couldn't get through my young little girl life without being labeled something, no matter what. Shortly afterwards, we moved from Watts to Inglewood. The other side of town was a little more diverse, so that was mostly the end of the labels, the name calling and teasing. I was glad that it didn't follow me. Now I was free to shed the thin skin for a thicker one. A new neighborhood, new surroundings, and a new quest helped me to venture on and escape my sad former years.

Junior high and the first two years of high school, I went to Lutheran schools. At some point my parents decided to re-budget and send me to public school. I managed to excel once they enrolled me into Morningside High in Inglewood but when I stop and think about it, I wonder why I wasn't thinking at all. How is it that I wasn't thinking? Well, to begin with, I overlooked a music scholarship that would have changed my future and instead chose to recklessly be in love (didn't see the big picture). High school offered me many opportunities to have a promising future. Things were looking up for me and I was involved in everything and every activity: varsity cheerleader, commissioner of activities of my class of '73, vice president of my choir, etc. I was on a roll, but my parents were strict and too much activity meant I was away from their watchful eye. They started cutting back on how much I could participate, so I rebelled and trouble started between us.

I had one boyfriend in high school (that didn't last long), but he really was only a stand in for the boy I truly liked that was in the army serving a two-year term. My army boyfriend through his letters was up and down about our future together, so my high school boyfriend was there to make me feel I had someone to hang out with. However, my parents wouldn't let me date, so I had to sneak out many times, even for school activities. When I say "sneak," I mean out the window, have friends lie and say I was going to some kind of adult-supervised practice... you know the scenarios.

Once I returned home to find the window was locked, and I had to knock on the door. The next thing I knew, they took me to juvenile authorities, who surprisingly were on my side. After talking to me, they realized I really wasn't a bad girl; I just needed a little freedom to be involved in teen activities. I'd never done drugs (still have not used drugs to this day, I might add), didn't smoke or drink, and sex hadn't even entered into the picture. My parents were told if they continued to have such a tight grip on me, they could possibly lose me to far worse consequences. So, my parents did agree to ease up a little.

One of the first things they allowed me to do was go to my junior prom. I was ecstatic. I slaved over making my dress and even made my date's tuxedo, no less. Believe me, we really looked good. However, because my parents wouldn't let me go to the after prom party, my date took me home early and went to the after prom party with someone else...in the tux I slaved over. I was so hurt. I reclaimed my love for my army boyfriend because I thought he would never hurt me like that. In a later chapter, I'll tell you how wrong I was about him (the reckless love I just mentioned).

As a child the teasing was so bad, I guess I didn't notice the many stares then. But as I look back I know they were there because I remember my mother defending me, her child, against those who said I looked like I didn't belong to her. Today the many stares and questions continue. It seems people with curious minds (at least minds curious about my features) always also perpetually leer. Even now, when I'm out and about, I'm questioned about my ethnicity almost on a daily basis. Sometimes I wish I could just hire an advertising plane to follow me everywhere, with a ribbon in the sky gliding behind it. So all those inquiring minds that have to know can look up and read the message: "Leave Me The Hell Alone."

Problem was, the scar I received that very first day of kindergarten hadn't completely healed and the older I got the harder I embraced the need to prove myself to everyone, which I realized nearly too late really was such an unnecessary fate put on me. By the time I reached high school I'd become somewhat militant. "Black Power" was in my blood. I had to prove I was a Soul Sister who had soul that ran deep to the core, from the bottom of my feet to the roots of my hair. I used to make this joke when people asked what I was. I'd say "Let it rain and you'll know." Anyone who knows anything about a sista's hair knows if it gets wet, it will kink up quicker than she could put up an umbrella to keep it straight!

In high school I wore the biggest afro of anyone. My hair was so thick that, believe me, I didn't have to do anything to it but wash it, pick it out with an afro comb, and go. Didn't even have to tease it with a comb. It naturally would kink up and form the perfect 'fro, which we called the "Natural" in those days. I'm not talking curly. I'm talking "as kinky as they come" afro. In the old neighborhood, they'd call it "nappy." Even with my soul-sister affirming 'fro, my eyes threw off the look I was going for. I still looked out of place. Like the white 1970's sex symbol Bo Derek wearing her blonde hair in corn rows and braids. Cute but strangely off beat. Seriously different from the norm. From the back, I looked like everyone else on campus with a natural halo circling my head. I blended in well; until I turned around. Then face to face, you'd swear you just encountered Bruce Lee's sister with a big afro wig on.

If you haven't figured it out by now, I guess you can at least tell I had some serious issues with my look growing up. You see, I've been forced to struggle with an identity crisis all of my life. I was raised in the Los Angeles community of Watts, which in the late '50s and '60s was almost completely black. I also spent part of my formative years living next to neighboring South Central, with its largely black and Hispanic communities. These neighborhoods, though they are widely seen by others as ghettoes and "the hood," were home to me.

In my young, impressionable life, my neighborhood was the only place I knew. I was part of my surroundings. So what if my eyes were slanted. That didn't mean I was different. I am what I feel most in my heart: a black woman with a tremendous amount of pride because of my upbringing and my family's struggles, accomplishments, beliefs and devotions.

When there was teasing, most of it was at school. My neighbors and most of their kids treated me OK. However, there was still sometimes that sense that I was an "other," an outsider that would at the end of the day go back to some other neighborhood like little Susie, the Chinese corner store keeper's daughter. She used to come to my house and play with me. Yet, even I knew that she went home to another side of town when her dad's store closed.

I grew up with a big chip on my shoulders that I just couldn't seem to shake. Wonder why? Because everyone wanted me to be something else. Not someone else, just something else. Something that I had no idea about or notion that it even existed in my black world. I wasn't raised around any Asian people, and didn't even know any personally except Susie. Like many of the blacks and Latinos in my respective communities, my limited real-life exposure to Asians included only the ones that ran the corner stores in our neighborhood or the Chinese restaurants we frequented. For some of us, they existed as characters in those Kung Fu movies than ran on television on Saturdays and in a few movie houses around town. To a large extent, unless effort was made, the Asian shop owners remained the inexperienced "other" to us; and probably they felt the same way about the brown-skinned black and Latino people who came into their stores on a regular basis.

I knew I wasn't a Ching Chong China and I definitely didn't know Kung Fu. My parents were black and so was I. I tried proving my blackness each and every day of my life. I was just as black as anyone in my race and in my community. To me, my light color was only proof that black people come in all shades on a color palette called "The many colors of African Americans."

My father was a medium-brown man with wavy hair and my mother was as pale as they come. So fair in fact, that in her younger days she was mistaken as white. Her features, however, were those of a beautiful black woman. For most people, there was no question as to my father's nationality— even though I always thought he looked like a dark Hawaiian. He was a big man with a full face that made his grey eyes slant a bit, just like mine. I wasn't different. All of my cultural traits were the same as my parents, so why was I questioned so often as to where I was from?

People would ask my mother when we were in line at the store, walking down the street, or just about anywhere, if I was "mixed with anything." Being an older mom, some would even ask if I was her granddaughter and question if it was her son or daughter that had the mixed baby. Plain ol' nosey people. Often, I'd see someone discreetly touching their eye with a slight pull while pointing at me, as if not expressing out loud their noticing the shape of my eyes would protect my feelings. Like they were letting my mother know they held some secret knowledge that I was different.   Bold people would just straight out ask what I was (referring to my ethnicity) and ask who she was to me. When I asked my mother about it she would always say, "They don't know what they are talking about. Just ignore their ignorance." Tight lipped and disgusted, she would not discuss it any further. It clearly upset her, but she never explained why.

As an adult I have at last come to terms with the revelation that we give others the power to impede our development. It's a power we so often use against ourselves. Sadly, it's hard to visualize how the weakness of our passion can allow us to connect with someone that has the ability to control our emotions, thus controlling our visions.

Amazing isn't it? You can spend a majority of time feeling like your world is flipped upside down because one person disapproves or decides for everyone that you don't fit into the world you so desperately want to be in. My advice: Snap out of it already!!! If you are going to let the power of one person control your destiny in life, let it be your own power. Do what you have to do to set into motion "Mind over matter." Get focused and visualize a path that will take you to a place where you are free to meet You and be You!

As you probably have guessed by now, I accepted the notion of my inadequacy at an early age. I always wanted to believe it wasn't my fault that I had adopted this destructive viewpoint and taken the abuse that came with it for so long. But truth be told, I waddled in it to the beat of my own disappointment that I wasn't exactly like others far longer than I had to. I was responsible for creating my own fate. I wouldn't let it go. Great and incredible things were happening around me and for me, but my acceptance of an old defeat overpowered any goodness I had going for me.

Don't let anyone, or anything for that matter, get in the way of what you should be for yourself. Don't let people's tiny opinions and ignorance beat you down to take even the smallest flake of your skin from you. Be strong and be in control. There's a little thing about love that I share with my children and grandchildren that I try to keep in mind with everything I do today.

One day, my youngest granddaughter Dylan was visiting me. She was about two and a half at the time. Out of the blue, she announced, "Grandma, I love you so much."
"Oh yeah? How much?" I replied.

She stretched out her little arms as far as she could. "Soooooooo much, I can't even reach" she proclaimed.

I held up my hand and put the tips of my thumb and index fingers together and pinched them as tight as I could get them until the blood went white beneath my skin. I looked at her, put my fingers close to her face and said, "Well, I love you this much."

She took it to mean I didn't love her at all. Her little face went sad and she had that bewildered look that demanded to know, Why? She knew I loved her. So, before she could ask, I explained by using the index finger on my other hand. I made a big circle with my fingers and softy assured her, "From this side of my thumb all around the world to this side of my index finger, I love you; and nothing can get in between my pinched fingers to ever get in the way of my love for you."

This is how we should feel about ourselves. Nothing should ever be able to get in between you and your love for yourself, your dreams and your ability to succeed in life. At times, I'd found it hard to let go of painful incidents in my formative years and past woes. Then one day it hit me like a ton of bricks.

I decided to take my own example about love, and at last took back the power. Today, I am the power of "ONE" that controls...Everything!

When I look back, I wonder how my good, loving, God-fearing parents missed the magnitude of my situation as a child. It could have been the influence of the era in which they were raised. Their parents believed nearly all things were taboo to openly discuss and hesitated to lay into controversial topics. Every discussion was always hush hush, from politics to sex talks. Things were swept under rugs so often that in time the dam rug had to be thrown away, because there was just too much debris to deal with. It is easy to see, then, why my parents didn't fully appreciate the dilemma I had faced and therefore gave me no assurance to build a positive foundation for my own self esteem.

My parents gave me everything except for a way to psychologically cope with the problem that grew inside my young mind. That thin layer of self doubt that swelled, soaking in all the negative karma from my name-calling schoolmates and other insensitive ignorant adults like a sponge. The wounds were never given a chance to heal because we never talked in depth about the hurt I suffered from the harsh words and judgments. So the scars from this absurdity basically festered there for years. I'm sure my parents' thoughts were that I'd grow out of it or that it would just go away in time.

Turns out the day did come when my parents decided it was time to seriously and at last address the issue. At thirteen, it was one of the most devastating days of my life. Not because of what they told me, but because of what they didn't tell me.

CHAPTER 2
The Little Lost Girl

I t's 1995 and I'm in the air, flying across the Pacific Ocean. The waters below me are calm, but it's getting dark and my view of the ocean is blurred. Interestingly enough, it's pretty much like my state of being: calm but blurred. There I sat looking out of the window in first class, seat 4A, wondering what lay ahead in the next few days to come. I wasn't in first class because I could afford such a luxury. As a flight attendant for United Airlines, I was entitled to the perk of being able to fly first class on any of the carrier's flights which I was not working. Particularly on this occasion, it was more than a perk to me. It was a gift. I sat back, relaxed, and enjoyed the ride. Of course, as an employee, you had to go stand-by and if you got lucky, you might get first class instead of coach. Business class was always a wonderful compromise if first class was full. This time everything was working in my favor except for the vexing task ahead and the long flight.

This was a journey I'd put off but could no longer

ignore. I needed to make sense of an emptiness I had felt for a lifetime now. I needed to do this once and for all to make me sane. I kept asking myself, "Am I making a mistake? Maybe I shouldn't tackle this, just give up and go home. Just let things be the way they are." No, I was bound for Seoul, Korea to find a little girl who had captured my soul and who I wanted to meet. I had to meet her. From the moment I became aware of her existence, she became a tugging force drawing me into her world. She needed rescuing and so I needed to find her and do just that.

I was told she had been in an orphanage such a long period of time, all she could do was cry. She was listless and withdrawn, malnourished and weak. Her paperwork said that with love she could be a healthy and happy child. Somehow, during the process to place her in the loving home she so desperately needed, she became lost. I was on a mission to find her because I wanted to love her. I think I believed that finding her would give me purpose and closure on my past and current issues. I could stabilize my self doubts and insecurities knowing her struggle was far greater than my own. I had to find a way to cure a long-suffering inner sadness, that sore that hadn't healed after all these years. A woe-is-me syndrome that had haunted me from childhood and popped up its ugly head from time to time. It needed to stop.

Those that knew me said I had so much going for me, there shouldn't be any reason to feel out of sync whatsoever. Nonetheless, I continued to beat myself up or at least project an image of an insecure person not focusing on the brighter side. I'd managed to put most of the sadness behind me, but as I was starting to get older and rumble through the memories of my past, I felt a sense of obligation to myself to understand why the road blocks had altered my way so often. My theory was if I could bring this little girl to a happier place to exist, I could bring myself to be happy with existing. Finding her was finding me.

While I looked out of the window searching through the darkness for anything to see, my thoughts kept rambling as if some answer would just manifest itself from the darkness, like in a thriller movie. I was hoping for something that could bring clarification as to why I was traveling so far from home to go on a journey that could turn out to be either enriching or very disappointing. No answer at all. Just miles and miles of darkness passing before my face. I couldn't sleep so my thoughts went deep.

Here I was, forty years old, ready for a change to happen in my life that could give me this purpose and stability I was in search of. Why? Maybe this could define me as a person, as a woman, that at last could end the quest to prove who I was. A black woman being forced to identify the double sides of her life, like a split personality or something. The side I was desperate to be and the side that I wished would go away. At least, that was how I thought and felt most of my life. So many had questioned and unfairly judged me all my life because of my look, my color, my hair. It was no wonder I had felt for so long like a dual, irreconcilable personality.

For a long time, all I knew was that I was an African American girl with an African American father and an African American mother. Both were proud blacks that raised me to have the same pride. I was taught that struggles were supposed to make you strong. The struggle I had made me weak, so much so that at times it broke me down with wasted years of feeling imperfect because I had allowed people to press me into an identity crises. I always seemed to be missing something. Something I needed that would project wholeness. I knew who I was but I wanted others to know and to just leave me alone, see what I saw and make no reference to the subject of race whatsoever.

Los Angeles is a melting pot of cultures and diversity that spans across the city. Yet today it still has its layers of separation, like the oils that float atop a settled stew. Over time, we've learned to mix and blend in; yet, there are still those times we have to struggle to hold on to our own identities because of issues at hand. A person can decide to dive into the mix, but she inevitably comes across those who have the NERVE to ask her to separate herself by staring at her and asking that invasive "have-to-know" question: "What are you?" Other times it is the equally divisive, "Where are you from?" In other words, How do you mix into this pot? As if they need that little bit of information before you're allowed to jump into it based on their standards or approval.

I know, I may sound a bit harsh, but you do get tired of the same question over and over again. Day after day. I just don't get why so many have to label you or identify with what you are before they can move on to having a regular conversation with you. The need to unscramble their minds in order to define you is so puzzling to me.

Maybe you've heard some of these frustrating, pointless questions. For example: "I hope you don't mind me asking, but I was just wondering, where are you from?"; "What's your background? Are you mixed?" I answer them. I start thinking, "Now what? What are you going to do with that useless bit of knowledge?" One doesn't go around asking people

"Are you white? Are you black? Are you a person?"
Often, I have wanted to shout back, "ARE YOU
SERIOUS?" I don't, though. When I am interrogated
in this way by such people, I give their feelings more
consideration than they give to my feelings.

But I do have my moments when I regress,
needing to overcome a few more obstacles still
lingering. I don't mind the questions so much when
I know it's part of an intelligent conversation and my
look is observed as unique or interesting. I just hate it
when someone from out of nowhere blatantly walks
up to me and throws the questions in my face. It feels
like a kind of credential check. Like "Hold on, hold on.
May I please see some identification before you pass
me?"

Having to deal with these questions all of my
life hasn't made it any easier to deal with them. In
fact, it has made me hard, defensive and stand-
offish at times. My past was marred by the tragedy
of allowing the powers of others to take away my
self worth with these questions, stares, teasing and
the constant need to know what my nationality is.
I still say, "Why?" It never even occurs to me to ask
anyone such questions. I look at a person and if their
race is not obvious to me, I really could care less. A
person is just a person to me and how he or she acts

or receives me is what matters.

Once I was out on a date at a crowded Houston's Restaurant in Century City, Los Angeles. It was a busy night and the restaurant was bustling and noisy, but still my friend and I attempted at indulging in a private conversation. Suddenly, a waiter (not ours) came up to me and though he was being polite, he said, "Excuse me, the cooks and some of the other waiters are all taking a bet, and we are wondering... what you are." I kid you not! That is exactly what he said to me. Out of all the people that were in that restaurant that night, how on earth did they pick me to run a bet on what I was? I guess I should have felt honored, but give me a break!

Before I could answer, my date, who was obviously irritated at the gall of this waiter, quickly spoke up, "She's a perfect lady. Now go take your bet somewhere else." As the old folks would say, "Nuff said." Looking up at him, I gave my date a thank-you-so much smile. I didn't say a word and the waiter tucked his head and went on. Curiosity killed the cat that day.

The boiling point for me when I decided I didn't want to answer the "What are you" question any more, was when a black man, a cashier at a local store, gave me a compliment. He said I was beautiful and asked about my background. I told him I was black and stated what I was often mistaken as. He told me I shouldn't admit I was black, because I didn't look it. If that wasn't bad enough, he then said that if he was me, he would be glad to tell people he was something else. I couldn't believe my ears. I was appalled and told him so. What a waste of my time. I was so ashamed of him and for him as a black man who didn't love himself.

My grandmother lived with us when I was a young girl and she questioned everyone that walked through our door as to where they were raised and what was their family name. Her reason and driving force for the questions was not to identify what you were, but to determine if you were connected to our family tree somehow. If your family was from anywhere near or around Shreveport or Franklinton, Louisiana, or your family name was Magee or Scarborough or sounded familiar to anyone else she knew, that just made her day. To her, it was like finding lost treasure and you were "in" as an addition to our family. Talking about her family tree was her pride and joy.

Grandmother, Mother Scarborough, we called her, helped me to see that we are all connected somehow. No matter how these connections split, the only questions we should be asking are questions like my grandmother's, to find out if we could actually be in the same room with a long lost cousin.

There were only a few hours left in the flight before I would step off the plane in Seoul, Korea in search of the little lost Korean girl. My oldest daughter, Kemarah, a family friend, Tita, and my then boyfriend and his brother were in tow on this journey. They were there for support in case I needed uplifting, should my findings be unbearable and I discover that little Lee, Yung Sook is lost forever; or on a happier note, in case I actually find her. They were there to cry or rejoice with me. Maybe do both.

I had plenty to think about, and the long flight had afforded me the time to do that thinking. I had to organize the search. Who was first on my agenda to call and how to get where we had to go. I'd never been to Korea, except for passing through once on my way to Hong Kong on a group tour (an interesting story I'll tell later). There was very little information to go on, so I was not quite sure what I was up against in this search. I had not researched anything. In fact, one day out of the blue I decided this was what I was going to do and the next day, I was on my way (although the thought of this day had always tugged at me). All I knew and hoped was whatever I was about to find out would change my life and those around me forever. I knew it. I could feel it.

We arrived in Seoul safely, settled into the hotel and planned our day. So that the whole trip wouldn't just be about business, although that was pretty much all that was on my mind, we mapped out some fun to add to the journey. Shopping and so forth. Anytime you venture off into something that is new and unfamiliar to you, there is a bit of fear that attaches itself to the situation. This was no different; the fear in me was dreading it. This was going to be hard for me because I rejected the idea of taking this journey in the first place. But when an urge takes control of your senses, sometimes you have to go with your instincts no matter how much you dread the task and the efforts it will take to achieve the overall goal to satisfy your yearnings. You send up a prayer that it is successful.

Thank goodness we arrived on a Saturday, giving me one more day to build my courage and settle my nerves because the agency I needed to go to was closed until Monday. When you go stand-by you have to pick the days when the flight loads are light. I'd previously looked up the flights for the several days before I wanted to be in Seoul and Friday was the best flight getting all of us there on

Saturday. Being there a day early, with an extra day to do nothing, we decided to get out and see Seoul. None of us had ever spent time on the ground in Korea before, so taking in the sights and shopping was probably just what I needed to get my mind off the day ahead.

I'd heard lots of wonderful things about the cheap shopping and how you could get anything made at the drop of a hat. It was all true. We shopped till we dropped. Kemarah, my daughter, a 5'10" beautiful twenty-two-year-old with wavy brown hair and a complexion so smooth and golden bronze you want to reach out and touch it to see if it's real, and Tita a few years older, just as tall and beautiful, were walking down one of the main streets. Suddenly a crowd gathered around them, pointing and speaking in Korean.

Of course, we weren't sure what was happening until they started taking out their cameras, chanting, "Moodels, moodels, you moodels?" in their broken attempt at English. The cameras snapped away and the two of them, who were not models, smiled for the cameras having a moment of wishful fame. I too was smiling with pride because there was a time in this country when Americans were not welcomed, and if you were African American, it was worse. You were an immediate outcast. So to see these beautiful tall black girls get this kind of attention from a whole new generation of open-minded Koreans thrilled me greatly.

The prejudices of the world have made most of us live through trying times. It's an uplifting experience to see any barrier drop even for a moment; but it was even more exhilarating watching my daughter and our family friend move through this idolizing crowd that saw no color, only what they thought were celebrities. However, I am in awe and disgust that everyone can't walk down any street and feel like they are a star in spite of their color. Too often in our communities, color determines whether or not we even make it down the street period.

After a full day in Seoul and a wonderful Korean dinner, we decided to call it a day and get ready for our real reason for being in this country. At last, I was finally ready. Being here now made me realize more than I had originally thought, before I took off from the States, how important it was for me to find Yung Sook. Every place I turned on the streets of Seoul, I got a glimpse of her face among the many faces I passed throughout the day reminding me that I had to do this. Find her. Know her. Know what happened to her and, most importantly, bring her home with me. Her face was everywhere. Her cheekbones, her smile, her curly hair, her color and even what I imagined her fears and sadness to be all about. I knew this sadness and fear and I wanted both of us to recover from the stigma put upon us. We needed each other.

I didn't have much to go on to find her, except a baby picture of her in a green paperback Korean passport that she had taken to come to America. Also I had only one piece of paper that was signed by officials giving a description of her sad little life. She was less than two years old with curly hair and tiny round features. In her picture she seemed sad and desperate to be loved. Her eyes, peering off the photo, seemed to plead, "Come and get me. I need someone to love me."

The excitement stirred though me all night and I couldn't sleep. Both joy and hesitation hovered over my dreams. I wanted so much to find her, but that desire alone couldn't open up ominous doors. Doors that hid a past I wasn't sure I was quite ready to handle. It's a big responsibility to open up your soul and let someone new into it. You just had to bond with the person, even if her world could possibly make your world become unglued. Oh well, so be it! I was going to do this and that was all there was to it. Like a brand new mom before she gives birth, the excitement and anticipation before she sees her baby for the first time still holds a bit of fear of becoming a mom in the first place. The questions abound: "Am I ready for this? Will I be a good mother? Will I know what to do or how to love my baby so it grows into a beautiful person?" Questions, questions, questions and the answers come after the fact when there is no going back on the realization that all of this is truly going to happen, ready or not.

Before daylight broke, I couldn't take the anxiety and excitement anymore and was up getting ready for the day ahead. Silently my heart was calling out "Yung Sook, where are you? I'm on my way. Get ready, 'cause here I come!" After all, I'd played hide and seek with this whole idea up to now.

This little girl had been ostracized because of the blood that ran through her veins. Cast out like me. I wanted to rescue her, save the little one and let her know she could be loved. The little I knew about her was enough for me to know her beginnings were full of despair and cruelty. With this, I knew how she felt and I knew her from inside out. I would later learn that what I thought I had in common with her was nothing like what I expected at all. In fact, I didn't end up being her savior. When I at last found her, she had already been saved by a force so powerful, it turned out I was the one who was rescued. So, the journey continued not knowing what was up ahead for me. An unexpected reveal would soon expose what I thought I had known already but really had yet to learn.

CHAPTER 3
I'm No Barbie Doll

One Saturday morning in 1969, alone in my room as usual, I was sewing clothes for my Barbie and her boyfriend Ken. Making clothes for my dolls was fun. As an only child, it gave me something to do and a way to deal with my loneliness, plus show my creative side. Mama had taught me how to sew when I was very young, and by now I'd gotten pretty good at it. My grandmother, who was a seamstress and designer in her day, had taught her daughters. So my mom handed down the skill to me. I'd even managed to make more than a few dresses for myself by now.

Actually the first time I made my own dress, around 1966 when I was about nine or ten, was the same time my father decided he never wanted to buy me a dress from a store again. Daddy was proud of my dresses and encouraged me to make as many as I liked because it meant he didn't have to go out and buy as many as I claimed I needed. He was soon retiring from his very long teaching career and wanted to cut back on the shopping Mama and I were used to, though I can't ever remember his denying her anything she wanted ever. I remember it was close to Easter and, of course, every Easter it was a must to have a new dress, new shoes and all the matching accessories. Daddy sat me down and informed me that, this year, I was allowed to get either a new dress or new shoes but I couldn't have both. To me that was unheard of. What is a new dress without new shoes on Easter? It's called being spoiled!

Anyway, everyone knew a new dress and new shoes were a package deal. Come on. After all, one without the other was certainly un-saintly, like an angel without her wings, to say the least. So I made a deal with dear ol' dad that I would make my own dress and then he could buy the new shoes to go with it. Well, he was thrilled when it was all said and done, but my mother was furious with me in the end.

I was so happy Daddy said I could make my dress, I set out to find just the right fabric and looked through piles and piles of remnants left over from some of my mother's projects. There was a trunk full of dresses with missing sleeves, zippers, and buttons. There were some dresses that had been cut out but never sewn and lots of bundles tied together for later sewing. There was nothing I could use right now. In the mix I found many patterns and pieces of patterns. Mother had taught me to make my own patterns from newspaper or paper bags, so there was no need for any of these. I'd make my own. Problem was I couldn't find fabric I really liked. From the pieces I did like, there wasn't enough to make a dress.

I hadn't bothered to ask my mother for any how-to instructions or to even help me for that matter. I wanted it to be a surprise. It was going to be my dress, my creation, and I didn't want her to get any credit for my new found ambition. Since I couldn't find what I was looking for in the remnant drawer, I decided to keep looking in the cupboard for anything I could use to make my new dress.

Standing on a small house ladder, I began my search of the cupboard. I searched for a long while, until, finally, I found my fabric. It was way in the back of the top shelf, stacked neatly with a bunch of things I never saw Mama use before. So, it must have been way up there for a reason. It was old and unwanted. That reason made sense to me. Mama must have hated these things because I never saw her ever use them and they seemed as if they had been there forever. Some of the things were wrapped in plastic and some had even turned yellow because they were just plain old.

I reached deep into the stack and pulled out the most beautiful white pillow cases with a lovely pattern of powder blue embroidery that also was woven to finish the scalloped edges. I held it up to me. "Perfect!" I thought. This was it. Shifts were in so all I had to do was cut out a neckline and some arm holes. Voila! My new dress. I made the dress out of one pillow case and the pockets, trimmings, a matching purse, and a head band out of the other.

My dad couldn't believe his eyes when I walked in with my new dress on. He ended up buying me a pair of powder blue patent leather shoes and baby blue fishnet stockings that had just hit all the stores in an array of pastels. My outfit was complete. Daddy was so proud of me. My mother on the other hand hit the ceiling. I do believe that from that day on she never forgave me until the day she died some twenty years later. From what I can remember, it was the start of her disapproval of everything I did from that point on. It turned out those pillow cases were bought on her honeymoon in Italy and she had taken great care to preserve them as a memory of that trip. As proud as Daddy and I were about my dress, I'm sorry I upset my mother. Her approval was very important to me. But, Oops. Who knew? If I had to do it again, I know I would have asked for her help and included her in my glory.

By 1969, I had decided it was time for me to stop playing with Barbie dolls. Not so much because of my age, but because it was my personal belief that I was too mature to continue fantasizing about what I imagined myself as wanting to be. A living doll. A black one, no doubt. I could only hope and pray everyone else saw me as one. Tall, with limbs that went on forever; big boobs, or at least perky ones; and long and flowing hair. I epitomized truly every young man's desires.

I imagined a perfect life to go along with my perfect looks. I'd have an abundance of high fashion clothes, accessories and definitely the perfect Ken beside me. Looks were important to me now that I had just crossed over the teen line. I had already been kissed and had started my period three years earlier. I thought I was grown and knew everything. So why was I dressing up these stupid dolls? They had been my playmates for a long time and the only things I really felt I owned. As an only child, they were inevitably the friends I could have anytime I wanted.

It was early in the year, too cold to go outside to find someone to hang out with. By now from time to time, a few neighborhood friends would come around if they didn't have a better offer or better option to keep them entertained. There had been no knock on my door today (and I was never allowed to go into anyone's house), so I stayed in with nothing else to do. I was deciding whether or not I should keep on pretending or just let my faithful friends get back to just being dolls. It was decided for me when I heard my name being called from the other room. I quickly gathered Barbie's items that were scattered across my bed, as if I were afraid to be caught dead in this world of make believe at my age. I knew deep in my heart I'd never see that world anyway. This was my own private little secret. I heard my father call my name again. This time I answered.

"Just a minute!" I yelled out making sure not to sound like I was "yelling" back. There was a difference, you know. It was all in the tone of your voice that said you weren't necessarily *talking* back; just clearly answering to a call you knew you'd better hurry up and reply to.

I quickly stuffed each piece carefully into a big shoe box that had once belonged to my dad. Months earlier I had recycled it from the trash, then wrapped it in some really pretty paper left over from a wedding gift I had helped my mother with a few days after retrieving the big box. I was always decorating something. So I turned this box into Barbie and Ken's stowaway home. It was kind of like my hideaway, too. A place I needed to go even though I was way too old to even be in the vicinity of make-believe.

I slid the box under my bed and as I stood to go see why I was being called, my reflection in the mirror caught my eye. It stopped me in my tracks. Standing there looking at the familiar stranger I began to wonder what happen to me that fast. Minutes ago, somewhere in my imagination, I was all the things Barbie had been and now a silly trick was being played on me. My limbs had turned into short and slightly chubby arms with legs to match. I completely went flat in the chest. Although my hair was long, it wasn't straight and flowing. My color was pale (yellow, they used to call it). There was no Ken standing next to me to escort me to the next room where at the time, unbeknownst to me, the truth about my real identity loomed.

I didn't have to ask my mirror who I was and what happened to that shapely black beauty. I soon would be told. I would find out my world was about as far away as you can get from my Barbie's world. I would feel for the first time in my life what it felt like to be slapped in the face and have everything you've known change in the twinkling of an eye. I found myself in a different world altogether. I'm certainly no Barbie doll and far from any wishful imagination of her. Surprise! I might as well had been everything those kids teased me about being in grade school because I wasn't what I told them I was all those years. I was different after all!

Dashing into the dining room, I feared I had taken too long to respond to the summons but the tone that had called out my name the second time was calm and assuring. I was not in trouble. I could see something was up, though. My father was standing and my mother properly seated near him with her ankles crossed. He looked like a king reigning over his queen. Actually that describes their relationship well and pretty much sums up how it was most of the time. My father adored my mother and would do anything for her. She, in turn, was quite loyal to him in every sense of the word, not letting anyone do anything for her king without her approval. She'd seen to his every need herself, and—in most cases—disapproved of anyone attempting to relieve her of her duty as his honorable wife.

Mama had taught school before I came along, but once I arrived she gave up teaching to be a stay at home mom and housewife. Her devotion to my dad as a housewife was serious. So much so, that she wouldn't even allow me to do much of the housework because that would have taken some of her glory away from her efforts to show him how wonderful she was at her job. I was never asked to do much around the house when growing up, so my father took me outside to help him do chores in the yard. I learned to mow the lawn, lay sod, build things and work on projects the way men teach their sons. The only thing I was allowed to do in the house was help my dad wax the hardwood floors and dust. Occasionally I'd get paid to scrub the bottoms of pots. Daddy called it using elbow grease and the more I used the more money it was worth. I had to negotiate the value of my shine, so I worked on those pots until I could see myself inside the pot all the way around to the bottom. Daddy also paid me to shine his church shoes. I learned to spit shine them to perfection.

Every summer we had great vacations, but my favorite ones were when we went to Oakland. My mother's brother lived there with his very large family. It was so great to visit my cousins and it seemed like they knew everything and were free to hang out in their neighborhood. I always felt so little compared to them; not because of my size but because of the self-assuredness with which they seemed to run their house and the streets. Not in a bad way, but in a know-how-to-get-things-done kind of a way.

On one visit, my cousin Toni, the tiniest of the bunch, cute as a button, with big round eyes and a deep voice, was ironing her shirt and shorts to get ready to go outside. She was about ten (I was a year younger). I remember my father being impressed and asking her to teach me how to iron. She was surprised I didn't know how, and from there she took me under her wings and not only taught me how to iron clothes, but how to do many things. That included how to keep up with her in the streets as we made our way through her neighborhood to hang out with her friends. I always felt like she was my sister and still do today. We had so much fun.

Thank you Toni, for always being my sister and teaching me so many useful things.

My mom not only taught me how to sew, she also gave me my first piano lessons. In my early years, I remember her sewing quite a bit and playing the piano on many occasions. Later, when everyone started praising my sewing and music skills, she stopped sewing and playing at all. At first, when I was about nine, we both played the piano at my father's church. She played for devotion and I played for the choir. One day in the year that I turned twelve or thirteen, she decided that since the members liked my up-tempo beats so much, a style that she just didn't want to conform to, she would abandon playing altogether. She wouldn't adapt to a style she considered too contemporary for her gospel taste or traditional hymns style. Instead, she'd take a seat that no one could ever take from her. So, I became the pianist of our church, and she sat in her glory as the wife of the pastor of Christ Full Gospel Baptist Church, of which my father was not only the pastor but also the founder.

Someone in our family once described my mother as peculiar. She was a very kind woman, it was said, but she never reached out to be your buddy. She was friendly, but not friendly enough for you to feel you could fully embrace her. She certainly didn't embrace others easily.

In recent years, I had a conversation with two of my cousins about my mother. Both had a completely different story to tell about Mama and how she did or didn't make them feel welcome. My cousin Carole and Sister Gaynelle were from Atlanta. Their mother (my mother's sister) wanted them to have the experience of going to school somewhere else. Gaynelle came to stay with my mother and Carole stayed with my Aunt Johnnie (another of my mother's sisters) across town. Carole's experience was great and she went back to Atlanta with a great experience behind her. Gaynelle, on the other hand, found her visit to LA a disappointing challenge. Mother didn't quite have the warmth and welcoming spirit that Aunt Johnnie had. Gaynelle's report when she returned home was the total opposite of Carole's.

At church, she was a great pastor's wife. Not remembering this detail, I was told, however, that when she and my father went to see the many people he was always visiting as a minister, mother always sat in the car. Never went in. Just sat in the car. Even when he visited my aunts on his side of the family, she sat in the car the whole time. Strange. I never got the idea there was any ill feeling looming about. In fact, everyone seemed to respect and accept her; but it seems that by her personal choice, she held her distance from most.

But she was very close to her own family. She looked up to them. I grew up with her making reference to their accomplishments and praising my older cousins for the degrees they were receiving from the top schools in America. She was impressed. I looked up to them, too, and wanted to be just like them. We also visited them often. She never learned to drive, so my father took us everywhere. Believe me, he didn't sit in the car when we went to see her side of the family.

Mother was very talented, and to this day, I'm not sure why she was a bit timid at times as if she was unsure of meeting people's approval. Oddly enough everyone struggled with meeting hers. I know I did. I sought her approval constantly and don't know if I ever really got it. She'd always tell me I did well. However, trailing that affirmation was always the ever so hated "but..." or "next time you should...." Never, "That was wonderful" or "Great." I was never sure if she was proud of me or not.

I hate to be hard on my mother because I know she tried in her own way to do her best by me. So why do I feel like I did nothing perfect enough for her? My best was never good enough for her. Oh well, I loved my mother. It may not sound like it, but I did. I have to admit, it's because of her that I started becoming a perfectionist. She helped me to do everything with a discerning eye and not to miss one little detail. Details mattered to her and I wanted her to be pleased with me, so I always dotted my I's and crossed my T's. I was always reminded to speak correctly. I had to clearly pronounce the endings of all my words (the t's and the ed's had to be heard) or she would quickly correct me.

Perhaps because she was a teacher, a good teacher, she had her way. The two of us made all of the art work for the church and even for my father's classroom billboards. It was the one thing we enjoyed doing together. When I think of fun with my mother, I have to think of the many projects we worked on. The Easter baskets we made to give away to hundreds of homeless children. The many arts and crafts for vacation Bible school. The little handmade dolls she used to make for me that were the most adorable dolls I had ever seen. Too pretty to play with, we'd wrap them in old sheets and store them away. I wonder whatever happened to those dolls?

She taught me so well, in fact, that my first professional job was teaching. I was from a family of teachers. Dad, mom, my aunts, uncles and cousins were all teachers. I said I would never teach, but of course, I lied. Mother had taught me to sew so well that the skill came in handy when I landed my first professional job teaching a sewing class at a high school in Inglewood. Later I worked in the garment industry for over ten years, doing everything from sales and merchandising to designing for new designers. I even had my own line for a short time, selling to major department stores in the western states. I walked away from my design studio and business when my mother passed. I wanted to explore the idea of living somewhere else besides California.

Even after more than thirty years of marriage at the time, my parents still were totally devoted to one another. I was my father's girl. My mother tolerated me. I do believe over the years, in her mind, I got in her way of being his soul and sole mate (as if that was at all possible). With no siblings to share in the family tree, I could have easily felt like "Two's company and three's a crowd," if it had not been for Daddy's vision for me to be around and actively be involved in his dream to have a family with children.

Mother was quite the proper lady, poised, refined and beautiful with long, silky, salt and pepper hair worn most times in a neat bun in the back of her head. Her skin was very fair in color. You almost had to look twice to notice she was a black woman. She was quiet and rarely exposed her emotions other than the disapproving tight-lipped smirk she'd give out when she felt crossed or uneasy about something. Always neatly dressed in the finest Daddy could afford, she was known for matching everything to a "T". That's how she dressed, in perfectly matched shoes, gloves, hats and jewelry to offset a beautiful suit or stunning dress. Her forte was her artistic ability and being a homemaker, she made many of her things. She grew up a society girl from Louisiana and was a Southern University graduate. I guess I'm to blame for her giving up her teaching career, but she continued to teach

Sunday school and was the pianist at our church until she passed the torch to me.

Mostly, she was proud to be Mrs. Robinson, Reverend Robinson's wife. Of course, because of me, she was also a mother. Her full name was Shirley Irma Dean and she was known to her side of the family as Auntie Dean and as Aunt Irma to my father's side. No one ever called her Shirley other than a couple of cousins that were named after her.   She had a soft loving way about her, but if you knew her you just didn't feel she loved anyone but my father. I can't remember her ever kissing me. When she did reach out to kiss and greet, believe me, her lips never touched your face. Actually, you didn't even get a touch of her skin at all. It was all just a gesture that she was trying to be cordial. If you shook her hand, within minutes, she went off to wash it promptly. Mother always had a hankie or tissue in her hand for just that reason.

As close as my parents were, I can't remember seeing them touch or share romantic moments more than a few times. I witnessed occasionally my father putting an arm over her shoulder. At night, from time to time, I would see him brushing her hair before bed. It was the only connection I can reference, but everyone knew they were deeply in love. If you saw one, you saw the other, if not beside each other then at least not very far apart.

Daddy was the most remarkable man I have ever known. Not because he was my father, but because he was truly in every sense of the word a man of God and a man that cared for everyone. He was a man of prayer and faith. He'd pray before we left home and he prayed when we returned, gathering us in a holding hands circle. This was always part of our daily routine. If he visited you in your home, at the end of the visit you definitely would find your household standing in prayer in the same type of circle. He prayed over everyone and everything. A vested school teacher and Baptist minister, he was a people person.

My fondest memories of Daddy were the many nights we'd go out on the porch of our Spanish style stucco home, painted flamingo pink with banana palm trees perfectly planted in front. When my cousins would visit, mostly in the summertime, we'd play on the always manicured green grass while Daddy would look up to the stars and meditate. Sometimes in the summer while he would water the grass, we'd run under the cascading water he would spray over our heads. Then without looking, he would pretend to accidently shower us with a rainfall. All the neighborhood kids would love to play in our yard. I think they would sit in their window and anticipate Daddy, or Uncle Ewing, as everyone called him, coming out to play with them. Seems out of nowhere children would just appear, and before I knew it I had to share him with a bunch of kids.

I'm not sure how to explain how children and teens alike were always around my dad, but very few of them were my friends or playmates. I seemed to always be joining in with the fun others were having with my dad, not the other way around. When my parents gave me birthday parties, it was my father who gathered the children together to attend.

If I had a complaint about anything he did, it would have to be when he'd turn my playtime into a Bible class when my few friends did come over. But what was strange to me was that my friends loved it (probably because he'd give us treats when class was over or walk us to the nearby park). Other than that, Daddy was flawless as a person and that's an understatement. His calm demeanor, charming mannerisms, welcoming smile and spirit made you at peace no matter how much your world was turned upside down. Daddy was always the optimist.

His slanted smoky gray eyes matched his silver

wavy hair that receded deep off his forehead. I had watched him many times slick his hair back with a wet, skinny, silver barber's comb. His smooth, glowing cocoa-toned skin gave him the look of an islander that baked in the sun every day. He was a large man that struggled with his weight. Doctors had warned him on many occasions to lose weight or his health would be at risk. Truth is, his prayer was that in his final days he would not have long suffering when he died. In his mid sixties he had a fatal heart attack and never spent a day in a hospital bed. God peacefully took him.

From his pictures as a young man, anyone could see Daddy had been as fine as they come. Somewhere early along the way, though, he had put on enough pounds to struggle with being heavy the rest of his life. Perhaps it was when he began his ministry and started eating all those amazing church dinners. For me his size was just more to love and that I did.

For more than thirty years, Daddy taught at Grape Street Elementary, located in the deepest part of Watts. He was still teaching there when he finally retired. This is why we lived in the community, because Daddy wanted to live where he worked and give back. He was the first black person to graduate from Pepperdine University in the '40s, which was his proud legacy. He wanted to work where he felt the most needed. Daddy was loved by all.

One wouldn't just meet him and go his merry way, Oh no. Daddy had a way of getting to know you and getting you involved by bringing you into his world. He became your friend, your confidant, your minister or simply Uncle Ewing as he was referred to by our entire neighborhood, family and friends. Uncle Ewing to many, Rev. Robinson to most, and Daddy not only to me but to some of my cousins who were close enough to call him that.

Today it was just me, their only child, they had called. For what I wasn't sure, but here I stood before them both. My father was dressed in his everyday wear. A dress shirt with a loose tie hanging around his neck. Dark dress slacks that probably belonged to a matching suit coat somewhere in his limited closet. A minister's closet. Moderate and always professional. Mother dressed in a soft floral dress that complimented her small frame.

I'd just turned thirteen and up until then, I had not been much trouble. At least I didn't think so. Normal things, you know, but always respectful. As the pastor's daughter, I had been a good girl. Up to this point I had never lost sight of that and knew what was expected of me as an example to the youth at our church. Maybe because I was the pastor's daughter, no one ever teased me or made fun of me there. I was totally accepted by all and to my knowledge known only as the pastor's daughter. Of course I played the piano so I was also the pianist.

"Take a seat young lady. Sit down, we have something we want to share with you." Daddy said. It was not a demand, but his tone suggested certainly I should do so. He stretched his large hand toward a chair that had been pulled out from under the dining room table for me so I could face them.

"Yes Daddy?" I looked at him with an inquiring look. I thought, Yeah? What do you guys want? I would never speak something like that aloud. Mother never tolerated slang or lazy talk. You had to speak proper English to her or she'd make you feel like less of a person for speaking improperly. Anyway, I just wanted to get this over with so I could go on with…oh I don't know, whatever an only child does alone while mostly wishing not to be..

Daddy had the same look on his face that he wore when he was getting ready to fire off one of his God-sent sermons to his congregation. I looked around the room to see if any of them would appear. No, no church member here to witness, judge or glorify me for that matter. Over on the big oak dining table where many Sundays those church folks I was just looking for sat and ate after morning service, feasting at our house before going back to an afternoon program or evening service, lay a Bible. Not unusual, but I noticed it was accompanied by a small stack of papers and a neatly folded child's dress. I had never seen it before. The little green and white gingham checkered dress couldn't be for me. Anyway it was tattered and discolored. Something to add to my fabric collection? No, I hoped not. I didn't want that old dingy thing.

Then it occurred to me. Oh, I thought, I get it. The dress had to do with a mission to give to the needy or something like that. Yes, of course. We were always doing charity work. Every year my parents gave me the option to either have a birthday party in November or have Christmas presents under the tree. I couldn't have both. If I wanted a birthday party, I couldn't have the floor covered with presents for Christmas. It was always up to me. I'd pick which one I wanted that year, and the money they would spend on the other went to charity, to the less fortunate. My parents wanted me to never forget there were children who didn't have the wonderful things I had.

My parties were always elaborate. I'm talking ponies, Ferris wheels, clowns and a feast for a little princess and her guests. Can you imagine a circus on your own front lawn, right in the middle of the ghetto? Looks like somebody on our block had it "going on" as one would say today.

Gifts under the tree were plentiful. I always wondered what the children got with the money we sent them every year. They probably were glad to have a bed to sleep on and food to eat. We had already had this conversation, and I was getting too old for parties like that. I was at an age that I wanted music and dancing; but of course, that was impossible. Whoever heard of a minister throwing a house party where teens could dance the night away? Sacrilege.

"Sit," Daddy repeated. I was still standing. "We have something to tell you." This time there was a demanding tone in his voice. I sat.

"Many years ago…," he began, and I felt some relief. Whew, I thought, it's not about me. I wasn't around many years ago. The question crossed my mind, though: How many years ago?

"We prayed many years for God to bless

us with a baby…" Before he could finish, I tried at guessing.

"Me?"

"Well yes, but before your time. We prayed and Mama was pregnant," he continued.

With a puzzled look on my face, I listened quietly waiting for him to continue. I couldn't believe my ears. I was about to learn about some older sibling I never knew I had. My mother never looked up, as if she was ashamed that he was about to disclose something about a brother or sister I had that ran away for some unknown reason. Turns out that wasn't it. So much for guessing.

"God knows what's best and that child was never born. The baby never developed and Mama was never able to have any more babies after that."

"You mean after me, right?"

"Well, God works in mysterious ways and when we lost one, many years later He gave us another."

"So she was able to have another baby later? Me?" I again questioned, just to keep it all clear in my own mind.

Mother kept her head down mostly and said nothing, occasionally looking over at me to see if I was following the story. She never said a word. That was just like her; she never had much to say. Her reserved manner left everything up to her husband to handle. When she did look up, I tried to make eye contact with her to see if she was for or against this talk. I looked over to her hoping to read her now. Nothing. She kept looking down as if hiding something or maybe she wanted to avoid the conversation altogether. It was clearly Daddy's idea we were having this meeting. Deep inside somewhere, I knew my mother loved me. I was quite sure of it, in fact; but it was my father's way that always assured me I would get the affection and love I needed. I looked back to my father's eyes. Something was heavy on his heart, though he was smiling.

"Mama never gave birth to another baby, but God allowed us to choose the baby we wanted. You were chosen to be our daughter, and you were blessed to get us as parents who really wanted you and love you very much."

At only thirteen years old, I knew I didn't know much about sex or child birth and all of that. My parents ran a pretty strict home and what I knew about these subjects was what I had heard from the neighborhood kids. What did they know? This certainly didn't make sense to me. How could my parents have had me without Mama getting pregnant again?

A year earlier I got my first kiss from a neighborhood boy. The second time he kissed me it was with his tongue, and I was terrified about getting pregnant. I guess I thought he could pass his sperm to my egg through kissing me. Not that I knew anything about eggs, sperm or any of that at the time. You have to understand, I had led a pretty sheltered life until then. These were the old school days and you just didn't talk about anything that was remotely connected to sex. This was before sex education in schools, so the talk about the extent of where babies come from or the many ways to make that happen if all else fails, was a talk you had with your mother right before you got married. So I thought. This wasn't possible, unless they were talking about the big A-word.

A couple of years earlier, one of my friends down the street told me her mother said I was adopted. When I told my mother about it, she simply told me, "People say many things that aren't true because they don't know what they are talking about. They should also mind their own business and not say things they know nothing about." Thinking back now, my mother must have been livid and called the neighbor to give that mother a piece of her mind because when I confronted my friend later, she denied saying such a thing.

Now here I was hearing my father confess it was true after all. My mother had denied it to me so many times that, after this day, we never saw eye to eye again. I hated that she and my father kept this from me. But mostly I was mad at her, because she was the one I ran to mostly for help when people bothered me about not belonging and fitting in. My father always said a prayer. To him, you had to have faith, and that would solve everything. If not, you're left questioning God. No one does that!

"You were adopted."

"Adopted?"

"Yes, we adopted you when you were just a baby. You were chosen."

Often, people ask me how I felt when I was told I was adopted. Truth is it wasn't the end of the world for me. The fact that I was adopted didn't upset me as much as one would think. My father said it perfectly, by saying I was chosen. Actually, that was great and I felt special. Being told I was adopted didn't faze me as much as what my dad told me after that revelation. The worst news was still to come.

Daddy reached over to the table, picked up some papers and handed me the one that was on top. It was a pamphlet, one of many I had seen from time to time. They came in our mail several times throughout the year. What did this have to do with me? I looked at the pictures and for the first time, suddenly realized that the children on the cover looked just like me. They had my color and cheekbones, chins and mouths like mine. But more than anything else, their eyes were the same as my eyes. These children didn't look healthy, they didn't look happy, and they didn't look loved. I had never noticed them before. As I continued to look at the pictures, Daddy was continuing with his explanation of the events that brought me into their lives. I was doing OK with all of this new information until I heard one word that totally upset me and pushed me over the edge.

"Korean?" I almost lost myself. I sat there with my mouth gaped open and a sour look on my face that said it all. I didn't want to hear this and I certainly didn't want to be this or have this problem. I didn't want to be like these children in the pamphlet. My interpretation of what he was saying and how he said it, sounded as if I had caught something. It didn't sound good and I wanted to get rid of it.

He said, "You have Korean in you and you are part black."

"What do you mean, Korean in me? What does that mean?"

I had never heard the word Korean and knew nothing about it. To me they were telling me I had something bad going on in my body. In spite of the smile on Daddy's face and my mother's affirming nods—like the ones you do in church when the pastor says something meaningful and you want to say Amen—I knew this news was unacceptable.

"Can I get rid of it? What's wrong with me?" I demanded, needing to know right then.

"It's not a bad thing to be half Korean. People come in all colors and Jesus loves all his...." I stopped him in mid sentence.

"No! Daddy, I need to know what I have to do to get rid of this. And what does half Korean mean?"

For the first time in this horrid meeting, Mama spoke up. "It's not a disease. Nothing's wrong with you. You came from another country called Korea. The people there are Koreans. "Orientals," she added. (Today we use the term Asian.)

"Oriental? I'm not Oriental and I'm not Korean either," I protested. It wasn't that I was prejudiced against Koreans, it was that I had no idea of the existence of such a culture. This was all so unfamiliar to me and in that moment I wanted no part of it. Home had always been my safe haven, and now here they were telling me every mean-spirited kid in grade school who tried to make me feel different, ugly, and foreign had been right. And I had been wrong. It all flashed back to me: classmates pulling their eyes tight with their fingers, the name calling, the seclusion, the ever so hated "Ching Chong China," the devil in the blue dress! Even the Kung Fu Terror was not what I wanted to be.

Daddy took back the conversation. "The program there (he pointed to the pamphlet I was still holding) is one we've been sending money to for many years because they have helped many children just like you find homes here in America. The Holt Adoption Program sent thousands of American babies left behind by GI soldiers. Babies that needed homes after the war. Many families were glad to welcome these little ones in their homes here in the United States. People that wanted to have a child like we did were very happy God sent them here."

Mama picked up the little dress on the table and the other papers. "This was the dress you wore when you came to us. I saved it for you and here is your passport that brought you to the States."

She showed me the green Korean passport. Inside was a picture of me as a baby, wearing the little dress. I looked so unhappy and scared.

"Take a look at these documents," she held the papers out for me to read, smiling like it was a relief to at last lay them out in the open. "These are your papers that told us all about you before you arrived."

I took them from her hand and began to read. At the bottom was the signature of a lady named Molly Holt. "Is this my real mother?" I questioned.

"No, but she is the daughter of the family that sent you to us."

"Is she Korean? Is that the family that didn't

want me?"

"No, they were a family that helped the many children come to America. We don't know anything about your natural family other than those were very hard times and many mothers had to give up their babies in order to give them better lives because Korea wasn't a good place for them to live back then."

"Daddy, I don't want to be from Korea and I don't want to be Korean."

"Well, God made us all and we are all precious in his sight. It's not where you come from that counts, it's who you are inside." Mama interjected.

"I can't believe this. I have your color Mama," I exclaimed, looking to her for some support. "I have your eyes Daddy," I turned to him for forgiveness for not being as black as he was.

"I don't want to be Korean. I'm black just like you guys," I snapped with a bit of an attitude, looking at both of them, imploring them to get it straight. All of my childhood, I'd had to prove myself to my peers. Now here I was trying to prove myself to my parents. I needed them to tell me something different than what I was hearing. The look on their faces said it all. It was true. There was nothing I could do about it and neither could they.

With the most ghetto attitude I could muster up, I let them know my disappointment on the whole subject and what I saw as a new absurdity. "I ain't from no Korea! I'm from Watts!" I asserted, as if that was the best place I could ever imagine being from. "Wherever this Korea is or whatever you say I have, you need to take care of it right now!" By then, the hurt pushed past the anger and tears began to slide down my face.

"You are our daughter and no matter if you are Korean, black, or any other race, we love you. God loves you. All people are God's people. When you came to be with us, you became one with us. A family."

As the talk concluded and we all stood, I remember having a big family hug and a prayer of thanks. But I was boiling inside and I was really mad at them. Why hadn't they told me all of this before now? Why did they let me go so long without knowing the truth? How many times had I come to them for answers? I knew in my heart that all I had just heard was true. But they just didn't understand.

For me that was the worst day of my life. The world I had known just crumbled in my face. My identity had been stripped and from that day, I changed. I was no longer whole. I had been split in half.

My parents had no idea what it was like going through all of the questions and the teasing, the long fight to fit in. Year after year, they had offered no explanation to help me with the taunting and the many staring eyes. For my entire thirteen years I had fought the fact that I looked different and tried my hardest to stand on the grounds that I was a whole black girl and as black as anyone in my community or family. I didn't want to be told anything different. I couldn't fathom the idea that I really was different from the people in my neighborhood, my school, and even my church and family. How could I ever face these people now?

If they had only told me something earlier, maybe I could have handled things differently. Maybe they could have said that we have Koreans in our family and taught me about the culture. It wouldn't have been a lie. I was part Korean and I was in the family. Right? They could have mentioned something about my heritage so it wouldn't have been such a complete shock. It would have at least prepared me for this day and kept me from being so afraid of the news. Instead, they watched me fight with everything in me to fit in, trying to keep anyone from making me feel bad about who I knew I was inside. Who I thought I was. I had to deal with everyone's constant questions:

"What are you?"
"Black"
"What are you mixed with?"
"Nothing!"
"Where are you from?"
"Los Angeles, Watts, 107th and Central."

No, this couldn't be. I decided then I would not accept it and I didn't. I grew up learning black values, I had black pride, and I clearly was a black girl. I had fought for it hard, and it was all I knew. I would just have to keep fighting even though I knew the truth. I didn't have to admit it. Not right now anyway.

I never talked about it again and I think I just ignored the entire ordeal. I buried it deep and didn't let it surface until I was ready to deal with it. Somewhere between the first day of kindergarten and my early adulthood, I got lost. Lost in not knowing which way to turn and lost in wondering which part of me to be. The part I looked like or the part I was raised as. One thing was for sure, I was a little girl that came from Seoul, Korea and grew up in the soulful ghettoes of Los Angeles. It was something I had to eventually accept.

CHAPTER 4
Finding Lee, Yung Sook

So here we were in Korea, a long way from Los Angeles, but interestingly enough the serenity in the air gave me a sense of tranquility as if I was surrounded by home. Literally I didn't know just how close I really was to the realization that home was closer than I thought.

After dressing for a chilly day, I got everyone up. While they got ready, I went downstairs to have some morning tea, hoping to calm my insides. Soon we were off on a local bus heading to the agency that would help me find Lee, Yung Sook. (In Korea the last name is written first.) The roads were busy with traffic as that of a big city. However, we saw many farm trucks with produce and livestock piled high en route to their next stop. Bicyclers and moped riders weaved in and out of the dense traffic, darting between cars, buses and trucks. It seemed like a sea of people on the streets walking and waiting for the lights to turn green. My mind was racing forward to how long it was going to take that bus to get me to my destination. Finally, the bus driver announced our stop.

There it was. I gasped as I read the green sign with gold lettering, attached to a big brick building. I stood under it and read, Holt Children Services. I had finally reached it. Much time had passed from the very first time I envisioned this day and I couldn't wait to get inside. With my heart pounding and my daughter and friends with me, I took a deep breath so I could walk through the door to find the lost little girl. First things first, I thought, "Take a picture." I took another deep breath, then I smiled a big grin and the camera captured me!

As soon as we entered, we were greeted by a lady who welcomed my crew and made us feel at home. I explained to her why we were there and showed her the picture of the baby girl I had in my hand along with the few documents. She took my information and led us to the records office, a small room with lots of record books in file cabinets. As she opened each drawer, my heart pounded harder and harder. I could hardly take it. At last, she took a book from one of the drawers and laid it on the counter in front of us. She opened the book and began flipping through pages and pages of orphans that were looking up from every inch of each leaf. There had to be hundreds of them.

My eyes started to well up and just before the first tear dropped, I saw her. There she was. Number 336. The same picture I had been carrying around with me, for a time that seemed like forever, was there among the thousands of faces in this orphan book. The face of Lee, Yung Sook, the little girl I came to find was right here in this book. We all just looked at each other, overcome with emotions.

Until that moment I never knew I would feel so connected, so at home with her. I hadn't wanted her to have an identity because it would have meant denying what I wanted to be within myself. She was a threat to all I had known, but now at this very moment it all changed with a drop of a tear to the page I was looking down at. It was the face of Lee, Yung Sook and me! We were finally one. United again. All that I was afraid of was lifted just seeing my picture in that book. It meant I was real. We were real. I had tried to belong for so long and hadn't figured out why I could never quite find my place. What I had denied wanting to be was before me. I'd fought hard against knowing this side of it because of that fear and now all of it didn't matter anymore.

Seeing myself in that book was the saddest yet most overjoyed feeling I had ever felt in my entire life. I was saddened at the staggering number of beautiful little children who ended up on the many pages of those orphan books. I was saddened realizing that I was one of them. Yet, I was overjoyed because I had found myself; overjoyed because I now knew I had everything to be thankful for. It made me realize how truly blessed I had been all along. How blessed I am now. I, China Robinson, had been rescued, saved by Lee, Yung Sook. I looked at the unhappy little face in that passport. Somehow, she was now smiling up at me as if to ask, "What took you so long to find out I was always with you?"

While I was sorting my emotions, being bolstered by my daughter and the friends we had with us, the lady that was helping us had instructed one of her coworkers to call the head lady at the agency. After a few moments, a woman with salt and pepper hair in nicely cropped curls, wearing big dark, round rim eyeglasses, walked in to meet us. She looked to be about sixty years old. The striped oversized sweater and loose fitting light colored khaki pants she wore gave her an appearance as a nun out of her habit. Being in Korea, she seemed a bit out of place as she approached me because she was the first white lady I saw here at a business. Her smile was very pleasant and warm.

"Hello, welcome. We don't get many orphan

returnees anymore, but we are delighted." She announced with a greeting. "My name is Molly Holt."

I opened my arms and gave her the biggest hug. By this time I had held back for too long on the flood of emotions and just let it all go. I cried full flow, snot and all. With no Kleenex or hankie, I used my finger tips for the tears, the back of my hands for the...well you get the picture. I showed her the adoption papers I had in hand and her signature at the bottom. It was the only name I grew up knowing besides my own on that paper. It was my only connection to Seoul. She was the Molly Holt I'd once asked my mother about. I couldn't believe it. She was the one that had signed my release almost forty years ago in order for me to come to the United States to be adopted by the wonderful family I had. It was her family that saved my life. Hugging her was like hugging my long lost mother.

Let me tell you how much this moment affected me; I am in tears right now as I write and tell this story. It's hard to hold back because I felt so lost and divided for so long and the day of this union meant I could go home whole, walking hand in hand with my newly found self.

Over the many years since the first time my

parents told me I was adopted and was half Korean or I should say "you have Korean in you" as stated by my father, I had gone from denial, to anger, to lying about it, to making up stories of my own and having fantasies about what if's. At last here I was embracing it once and for all. I could now welcome every aspect of this venture to take Yung Sook home with me. To let her be part of my world and try to understand hers. We were one and I found no need to separate her from my soul any longer.

When I was in my early twenties, I had once tried to totally accept and embrace the whole Asian thing and learn something about my heritage. I had decided to take it on with pride. But I really didn't devote much time to discovering anything about any of the Asian cultures. Seems I wasn't really ready to fully educate myself about it just yet. My attempt was only on the surface, so I learned very little. However, in this attempt to accept it, while going through a really bad moment in my life, I decided to change my name. I changed it to the name I had been called the first time I was teased. China. My family all wanted to know why. Why not?

I was on a musical road trip with Dakota, one of my close friends at the time, and we met a little girl named China. He said to me, "That should be your name." I told him, "It already is. I've had that name all of my life." So from that day on, I guess I renamed myself. I already owned it; I just needed to legally change it. China it was! After all, I'd carried that name with me since grade school and it was mine. It was kind of a nickname. Of course in the late '70s it was cool to give yourself an exotic name, something that identified you like a rebirth. If you were a Hippie, perhaps you would rename yourself "Flower" or "Peace" or if you were into Bob Marley and reggae, you might call yourself Rasta or like my cousin Herb who re-pronounced his name to be called "Erb"(still spelled Herb). For me it was China.

When I was adopted, my parents gave me the name they wanted me to have. My father's mother was named Florida Robinson. She played the piano. He wanted me to be named after her. My mother wanted me to be named Michelle. They agreed and the name Florida Michelle was created for me. I grew up Florida Michelle, but was called Ching Chong China so much, I think I answered to China far more than I answered to Florida. (I really don't look like a Florida.) Anyway, I'm sure you're surprised I legally renamed myself China since it was such a sore thumb for me. But it's my way of saying, "I can handle anything that comes at me and make it work for me." Finally, I embraced the name and made it my own. It also says, I'm at last OK with being half Asian. African Amerasian that is!

My mother flipped and my father never once called me by my new name. Other family members had to get used to it over the years. By now, I think everyone has gradually adapted. Today, if anyone walks up to me and addresses me as Florida or Flo, I know they are from way back in my past.

So I went from Lee, Yung Sook, to Florida Michelle Robinson, to China Michelle Robinson. In reality, when I look at all three names each tells a different story and each has its own life and identity. But, I proudly say, we are one. Three peas in a beautiful pod.

Eisenhower was in office for a second term and the Korean War had been hard on Korea and on America. Our American GIs came home leaving thousands of babies and children behind, offspring they never knew they had or had just forgotten. The aftermath of war doesn't just include casualties and disappointments. Young Korean girls and women, some of whom were prostitutes, hoped to come to America for a better life. Many found themselves giving birth to children that would never be accepted by the purity society of the old world, which would tolerate no mixed blood, as part of a complete systematical homogenous era.

Tragically, terrified mothers abandoned these Amerasian babies that were grossly ostracized. Most ended up in orphanages with bad living conditions. Many who didn't die from disease and sickness were found washed up on the seashores; their mothers killed them to save them from torture in the streets. Clearly Americans were hated and to have any mixture of their blood was proscribed or abhorrent. White American blood was bad, but black blood was like having leprosy. Whether the child had black American blood or white American blood, he was undoubtedly placed in numerous anathema categories. Half-breed. Reject.

In the fall of 1954, the Holts attended a "World Vision" (an outreach charity organization) meeting in Oregon headed by Dr. Pierce. It was there that they were influenced in hearing the imminent need to relieve the suffering and heartbreak of little ostracized mixed-race children. This rich American farmer and his family saw the urgency for a major rescue of these children and had the desire to give them a better way of life. World Vision had already begun setting up housing for thousands. However, Mr. Holt gave up his family's entire fortune to organize efforts which saved well over 30,000 orphans and brought them out of Korea. Their struggle to build Holt International Children Services (an adoption agency) is an amazing story that was more heart touching than anything I have ever read. It's one of the most remarkable and incredible stories ever told about selfless giving and love.

The Holts single handedly embarked on a journey to bring these unwanted little ones to America and other parts of the world, placing them in loving Christian homes. Each day their efforts came with seemingly insurmountable challenges and pitfalls. Some so tremendous that, even hearing about it some forty or fifty years later, your heart bleeds for the Holt family.

Walking in faith that God would give them the strength to endure their labor of love, they managed to find a way to place these children in the homes of empty nesters. Their unselfish giving and will to carry out a mission given by God created a new world for children up against the worst of odds. I sincerely urge you to read the story *Bring My Sons From Afar* by Bertha Holt, published by Holt International Children's Services (Eugene, Oregon). You will never complain again about anything. It is written like a daily diary of the struggle and hardships the Holts faced, and the courage, determination, and sacrifice it took for them to realize God's anointed work.

It was the Holts that fought to have an orphan bill passed that, had it not been rejected, would have allowed them to bring more children into the United States. Eisenhower wasn't strong on civil rights, but through his foreign policy he signed and passed the bill to assist these "war babies." Thank God, I was blessed to be one of those little orphans that were saved by that bill.

To my birth mother: Thank you for having the courage to take me from your breast and give me up. Thank you for taking the first step to save my life.

In the early '50s my American parents took in many children from time to time. Many of my older cousins had stayed with them at one point or another, but my parents wanted to have their own child to raise. My mother, unable to have any more babies, was encouraged by my father to welcome the idea of adopting. They went through great measures to fulfill this dream. Many attempts were made. Brown babies (as they were called) were a commodity and were hard to get during that era. After being denied over and over again, my parents decided to try their luck with an overseas program. They received and read many pamphlets about adoption, which they obtained through their missionary connections. They read about the many unwanted babies in Korea needing homes in America. This was the answer to their prayer.

On March 17, 1958, the long journey was over for a plane full of orphaned Korean children. They had traveled from the orphanage at Hyo Chang Park in Seoul, Korea and landed in Portland, Oregon to begin new lives with awaiting parents. I was one of those little ones. Lee, Yung Sook and me.

Although my parents were both in their fifties, they decided my father would take the trip to Portland to bring me to my new home in Los Angeles. The two of us arrived at my father's sister's home where my mother anxiously waited for us. But when I arrived she was afraid to touch me because my head was full of lice. It was my Aunt Kitty (Katherine) that bathed me, cleaned me up by combing the lice from my little curls, and fed me my first meal in America. My cousin Norma Jean, a teen at the time, recalls me holding my hands and not making a sound. She said I kept holding my little finger tips together and looking as if I didn't know what was going on, but when it was time to eat I really ate well. Mother was a bit timid about things like lice, so she needed a little help with the situation. My father was beaming with joy from the moment he saw my little face to the moment he walked through my aunt's door with me in his arms. Until the day he died, I was his pride and joy.

I had no idea when I was growing up how fortunate I was in having so many sources fighting against all odds to save my life. This gave me the tremendous opportunities to be and do whatever I want to be or do. Knowing what I know now makes me ashamed of all the selfish whining I did and all the needless fighting to be someone else. I now realize I was merely fighting against myself.

I was so extremely happy to have found myself among the pages of those books, that I really didn't need to find out anything else. Finding me and Ms. Molly Holt was all I needed to complete my journey at last. Ms. Molly was gracious enough to spend the entire day with us to introduce me to my entire story.

First, we toured the orphanage. It was now caring for many disabled and mentally challenged children and adults. Seeing the many little handicapped babies touched our hearts. Holding such precious gifts from God, Kemarah, Tita and I left having a new lease on life. Knowing how wonderful we had it back in the States truly made us appreciate everything we had to live for.

Later, Molly took my boyfriend and me on a three-hour drive north of Seoul to the small village in South Korea where I had originally come from. We discovered I had come to the Holt Agency because the little village orphanage where my birth mother left me could not take care of sickly children like me. My mother had not weaned me, and I became so depressed and sad that I would not eat. I became very sick and malnourished. I had lost my will to live. In order to save my life, I was brought to Holt by donkey on a two-day journey. It was the only means of transportation available from that village at the time. Hold on…two day journey, by donkey carrying a sick baby that wouldn't eat….God was with me….

Holt was more of a nursing facility than any of the other orphanages, so many babies ended up there and were saved from overcrowded and dilapidated housing. While touring with Molly Holt I was saddened to learn, through an interpreter, that had I not taken so long to accept the heritage I wanted to deny, I might have found my birth mother. The orphanage had turned into a small school and the new administration had burned the old records only a few years earlier. However, some of the same staff was still working there and one woman in particular remembered I was the only colored baby they had. She's the one who told me the story about my mother.

Now fully dressed in my new soul, my mixed sides as one, flying back across the ocean, my feelings were stirred about returning home. It was almost as if there was some confusion as to where home was. Over the past few days, I'd learned so much about the little life I lived in Seoul. It intrigued me to think, What if? I tried to envision myself in tears, with a runny nose, waiting for my mother to return. When she didn't, even as an infant, I guess I just shut down. Somehow, however, I feel as if part of my heart still remained in Seoul and when I returned, that heart reached out to me and welcomed me home. With everything I learned and saw, it gave me peace that now when I think about the world I never knew, I am connected to my birth place so differently than I would have ever expected.

The first time I saw the village, I remember thinking it looked just like the set of the TV show *M.A.S.H.* I was sure the little village looked like that the last time I was there, although I was too young to remember it. Soldiers still walked around with rifles strapped to their backs, guarding the off-limits grounds. A large section of it was gated with barracks and military trucks roaming about. It's no wonder so many villagers got sucked in. It was quite impressive to see. When I saw this, I tried to envision my birth father smiling out to me through the fences of the yards, sending out a chin-up to me that everything is alright now that I have returned.

Many times, I had been asked if I ever wanted to find my roots and it just wasn't important to me. Now I will always regret waiting until it was too late to find out anything about my biological family. It was now impossible to find my mother and without her there would be no way to find out who my father was. Funny (just a cute little memory), in my twenties, I had a thing for older men. Once I was on a date with a gentleman more than twice my age, sharing with him that I was born in Korea after the war. He then told me he was in that war and remarked, "You could be my daughter." That did it for me and I didn't date anyone else from that era.

Once I was on tour with my aunt's travel agency, Henderson Travel, as they were doing their annual Hong Kong tour. Many of my family members were along on this trip, including my adopted mother (our last trip before she died). I hate calling her that (adopted mother) because she was the only mother I knew (but for the purpose of this book, I want it to be clear).   We had a twenty-four-hour stopover in Seoul on our way to Hong Kong, not enough time to find out any information about my roots. Let me tell you, though, it was one of the most memorable vacations I ever had with my family. Before the trip a family friend, Senator Nate Holden — who was well connected to the Korean community in Los Angeles— suggested *Korean Times* do an article on my first trip to Seoul. I thought great and did the interview. I was told a Korean mother never forgets her baby.   If my mother was still alive, good chance she would recognize me.

To my surprise, when we boarded the Korean Air aircraft and settled in, one of the flight attendants held up the front page of the *Korean Times* and asked me if that was me.   There I was, big as day, front page news along with the little passport picture. The Korean Air flight attendant read the headline for us: "Korean Orphan Comes Back to Seoul to Find Her Roots." When we arrived in Seoul, all of us stepped off the plane with a group of Koreans that gave welcoming honors. They toured with us that day and gave me a traditional Korean dress. We had a traditional dinner and I left with books about Korea and a smile on my face, because I was a star for a day. I never heard anything else after that day, but I was happy to have been received so well.

Home is where the heart is, I've heard, and since I've felt split for so long, I can now say, I have a little bit of heart here and a little bit of heart there. What's great is the two sides of my dual identity have come together and connected in spite of the seas between my two halves.

CHAPTER 5

Vulnerable Acceptance

After becoming whole with myself, bringing Lee, Yung Sook home into my heart and soul, I had to have a real cleansing of all the negative feelings I had collected in my many years. Like an enema, I had to get rid of all the poisons from my mind that made me weak and vulnerable from as far back as I could remember. I wanted to find positive things in every experience I went through. No matter how bad it was. I needed to know that any and every experience meant something good, offered things to learn from and carry on as a lesson of what was positive or what to avoid in my future.

Our childhood experiences cling to us throughout our lives and move with us from one decade to another. If they are bad experiences, before you know it, if you're not careful, you've spent most of your life in utter turmoil. The good memories are hard to duplicate and the bad ones become hard to shake. We fall victim to our own fears of overcoming obstacles we've encountered. Somehow, we start to believe in our past woes, drawing strength on negative dramas, dropping deeper and deeper into believing we'll never come out of it.

What should be happening is you try to build on a mind set that you will not allow your strengths to be overpowered by your weaknesses, leading you to accept the negative. Don't rely on negative forces. Stop stunting your growing potential. Brace yourself, come to terms with what your weaknesses are, and decide you will pull up and out. Focus on raising your confidence level by assuring yourself you are worthy to be on a higher plateau.

Of course the need to be accepted was always my biggest weakness. I find that when you are seeking acceptance because of low self-esteem, you place yourself in unbelievable situations. Often I fell deep in that hole. Not once, not twice, but several times, in fact.

When you are in a vulnerable state, weakened by the inability to use good judgment, acceptance of others usually is not very selective. Anyone and anything goes. In desperation to be liked, your vision of people in general is blurred and you may see them as having an edge on life that you don't have. So, whatever they may be into, you are drawn in by default. I say default because your ability to not see clearly your own path or what you would chose for yourself usually will be so entirely different than when you look on someone else's map. Therefore, you allow yourself to be led by the strength others may have even if it's down the wrong road. You really don't care! Of course you know better, but at the time that's not a priority. Being liked and accepted is far more satisfying than worrying about your leader's intended destination or goals. You just want to be in the vicinity of someone that will take you by the hand.

I don't really know how many times I allowed myself to be led by these needless forces, only to discover they were a waste of my time. Though you do learn something from every experience in life, you may find you come out ahead even when it's a terrible mistake. However, you can't help but look back and realize you could have spent that time traveling down a more worthy path. An entirely different road certainly would have lead to higher ground where you could have really made something of yourself a lot sooner than riding on the trails of others. But, for the time being, you are being accepted by what you believe is a higher power and suddenly you are wanted. Desire to simply be included can make your crossroads unreadable and confusing as to which direction or path you should take. So you find yourself choosing to be led.

Unfortunately, when you become this desperate often you mistake your position as a friendly connection or—heaven forbid—LOVE. Most likely misguided love. You are now lost. Fact is, usually you end up just being used! Used for someone else's gratification in reaching their power struggle. Anytime you connect with someone because you need acceptance during a vulnerable state, believe me it's the wrong connection and you're definitely in the wrong place.

Truly, the hard part is recognizing you're desperate. In order to recognize you are in a vulnerable state, you must first come out of denial that you are even in this frame of mind in the first place. Look around yourself and ask these questions. Are you in a world where you want to be? Or are you in someone else's world? Have you mapped out your path? Or do you listen to other voices telling you where to go? Everyone wants to travel somewhere. It may as well be to your destination of choice.

I've been telling you the story of my childhood and how lost I got by being in a state of an identity crisis. I believe these experiences made me weak early on. I found myself bound for a life led by some really undesirable characters to say the least, because I wanted to fit in so badly. My judgments were blinded by the pure need to belong. I hadn't developed the ability to recognize. I was desperate!

My rebellion that began when I was thirteen, because I was so angry about finding out about my heritage, went on throughout the rest of my teen years. By the time I was fifteen, I was ready for an escape and ventured on to find myself in any form of acceptance available to me. Inevitably, I teamed up with someone else's misery and the two of us struggled with our insecurities together. By the time I was seventeen, I found out what misery really was. My appointed savior turned out to be over the edge, ultimately on the devil's side. And this was all because I never took the time to look on the brighter side of my story and see just how wonderful life was for me. I had given in to deception. It was written on the wall, but I ignored it and failed to see the signs that clearly were before my very eyes.

Captured by a bad situation, I found myself on the dark side. However, I was too close to it to get the message. So sad. It was easier to muddle through it as opposed to taking a moment to escape and discover what was a better situation for me on the better side.

My first real crush was a boy that went to my church. My father was the pastor and my crush's father was the assistant pastor. How convenient. A perfect union one would think. Wrong! With strict parents, I at first thought this was somewhat an answer to my prayers. I could be close to boys while I was right under the careful watch of their doting eyes. No chance of them objecting to my seeing, at the time, the boy I thought to be my one and only true love.

He had nine brothers, one as good looking as the next. It didn't matter which one you liked, there were enough boys to go around to every girl that attended service on Sundays. Each girl could pick a brother of her very own. And we did. Of course, I picked the one that really didn't like me. He was the oldest of the boys and a few years older than I was. I was about eleven and he was a "grown" fourteen, so he was naturally way out of my league. He didn't want anything to do with such a little girl. Oh well, I actually handled the rejection well and decided to shift my attention to one of the brothers closer to my age. No, he wasn't my first choice. But I thought that if I could get just one of them to like me that would be fine and dandy.

It took a few years of puppy love to make the true love happen, but finally it did and the younger brother fell for me head over heels. I fell for him, too. Something about him was all wrong and my mother knew it. She could see the truth in the signs that I read all wrong. I'd always felt she didn't like him because, as you know, she rarely approved of anything I did, and liking him was one more thing I did wrong. She made her feelings known, but I certainly wasn't going to let her stand between me and anyone who liked me back.

Both of us were from pretty strict homes and by the time we were well into our teens, we began to rebel against our parents. His situation got so bad, he decided to join the army to escape the madness, but not before he tried to commit suicide. A sign. I ignored it.

Although I was sixteen by then, my parents didn't allow me to date. So we had been sneaking to see each other. Soon we became very close, depending on our friendship and what we thought was love to get us though the tough times. On the day he attempted suicide, we were on the phone. I sensed something was terribly wrong. He began breathing on the phone like he was in a deep sleep, yet gasping to take each breath. I kept calling out his name to wake him and when he wouldn't respond, I panicked. I didn't want to hang up, so I ran to a neighbor's and used the phone to call his mother.

Their home was around the corner from the fish market his family owned. He'd said he was calling me from there. I should have thought that was strange, since it was after hours and the market was closed. Well, his parents rushed over to the closed market. There he was, lying unconscious, with the phone still by his ear and foam coming out of his mouth. He was rushed to the hospital where they pumped his stomach to remove the pills he had attempted to overdose on. Well, he recovered and shortly after that incident his parents signed for him to join the army. So, he went into the service for a two-year term.

Thing is, this first love of mine was somewhat of a loner in spite of having nine brothers. He clearly was the drifter of his family, needing someone like me to help him come out of his shell. I needed someone like him to make me feel wanted. We were a team holding each other up. Two crutches holding up pain in the middle. It's really sad when two desperate people merge their woes together and end up getting double trouble. He came out of his shell and I ended up in a living hell.

During the time he spent in the service, he wrote me often and in his letters admitted to using a lot of drugs. Another sign I ignored. By the time he got out he had gone from being a boy in a shell to being as mean as you can get. I knew he had serious problems before, but I ended up married to him before I found out he had totally lost his mind. He was a time bomb waiting to explode each and every day of our married life once the honeymoon period was over.

When he was in the army, through the many letters we exchanged, we started talking about getting married and having a family. I wanted a way out of a home ruled by parents that wouldn't let me do anything I wanted to do, so we started planning the wedding. It took place a few days after he was discharged for good. I was seventeen almost eighteen and he was a few days shy of turning nineteen. We were way too young for this kind of commitment. Neither of us understood what it was we were getting ourselves into.

I don't understand how my parents went along. My only guess is that I had become quite stubborn and rebellious by then. On top of that, during that era, many young girls from our church became pregnant. Perhaps it was a relief to marry me off before I had a chance to disgrace them. Of course, many assumed I got married because I had already turned on the oven. I'm sure everyone was counting the months following our wedding. They had no luck with that.

So, my parents gave in and his parents went along. The first six months we lived with his parents. That turned out to be the only time in our marriage we were somewhat happy. He was on good behavior to prove to my father and his that he was a responsible husband. When I got married, I was a virgin. In no time, however, I was expecting our first child. It was all happening so fast. What in the world had I expected?

I'm sure he felt the pressures of taking care of his new family and making a good impression on our families. But, my God, the boy just went ballistic at some point and became an abusive nightmare. He was mad and unstable all of the time once we moved from his parents' home and got our own little one bedroom apartment. It was a cozy little place in Santa Monica and cost us the princely sum of $200 a month.

We were both trying to work, go to school, and keep up with other responsibilities. He worked at the Veterans Administration while attending classes at Pepperdine University in Malibu (my father's alma mater – LA campus). The plan was for me to give up the idea of school for a while to have the baby. I attended some of his lectures with him and took his notes so I could help with his homework so he could get some sleep between work and school. In this plan, after he finished, I would be able to complete my studies. That plan failed miserably. He got good grades and I got beat up. Every day.

I can't remember the first time he hit me, because after a while it happened so often I just lost track. I can tell you some real bad moments. For the most part, I never knew when it was going to happen. I just knew it would happen at some point in the day. It's a terrible feeling, to have to tip toe around someone in order to keep them from exploding, knowing you are going to be the target of their blast. It's really like walking on a minefield, praying you don't hear that click, just before it goes BOOM!!!

Girls, young ladies, women, boys and men, if you are in a situation anything like this, move on right now. Believe me, there is nothing you can do to strategize your way through a minefield of abuse in which detonators are tripped the minute you see it for the first time. For those who say, "Well, my situation is nothing like yours," abuse is abuse and once it starts, it grows bigger and faster than anything you will ever experience. So big you will NOT find a way to control it. It will not go away! Therefore, you have only one choice and that is to quickly step away from the danger zone. For good. I know how hard it is to go. I know the fear. Believe me, I do! The sooner you go, the better off you'll be in the long run. So, go ahead and be your own s/hero. Step away and run, run, run and don't dare look back.

We were driving on the Santa Monica Freeway one Sunday morning, going to church, no doubt. We're riding along having a regular conversation and I happened to look to the right of our car where another car was passing. The driver winked at me. I don't know why, but I faintly smiled at him. It was the kind of smile that hinted at some concealed pain. I was thinking, "Oh, please. How rude." The next thing I knew, my lips were swelling faster than that car had zoomed past us. I felt like all my teeth were going to fall out of my mouth. My husband had slapped me with the back of his hand so hard I went dizzy. Our car suddenly pulled over to the shoulder of the busy, fast moving freeway.

"Get out of the car whore!" He ordered.

"What?" I struggled to speak, holding my mouth with one hand and my belly with the other.
"I said get the f— out and take your bastard

kids with you."

We had already had our first baby and I was about seven months pregnant with the second one by now. I struggled to get my little daughter from her car seat. I guess I wasn't moving fast enough, because he began pulling me out of the car by my hair as I struggled to release my child from her restraints. I pulled her in my arms just as I felt my big pregnant self get lifted out of the car by his heavy hands. My barely 5'4" 110 lbs frame was no challenge to his 6'3" 198 lbs physique.

When he released his grip on me, I hurriedly began to walk down the side of the freeway. I can only imagine now what the motorists who sped by the pregnant woman walking along a busy freeway with a toddler in tow were thinking. Just as I reached the exit ramp, one hand holding my belly and the other holding my child, my head hung low so no one could see my beat up face, I heard the car pull up beside me. He had circled around, getting off and then back on the freeway, to pick us up. Without a word, he opened the door and gave me a look not to be argued with as I got in.

Needless to say, we never made it to church. We went home to our little apartment, where there was no escaping his belligerent presence. God knows all I wanted was to have a little time to myself to cry. I dared not in front of him, as any little thing could set him off. So I stayed quiet, putting ice on my swollen mouth. As usual, after he calmed down, he told me how sorry he was while begging for my forgiveness. Thing is, with an abusive person, you really have no choice in the matter to forgive him or not, and he knows it. If you don't, it starts all over again because in his mind, it's all your fault anyway. You deserve it. So, you are too afraid not to agree with whatever he proposes. Your objective at that point is to live.

Once, and only once, I tried to stand up for myself and that resulted in the worst beating yet. I think I ended up on the floor of a tiny open closet that day, lying battered, naked, and terribly uncomfortable on top of shoes. With my fingers invisibly crossed, I forgave him. I don't even think he remembered why he was so angry at me. It didn't matter. He never mentioned it again and I didn't either.

His brothers weren't allowed to visit our house and my family was never comfortable dropping by. There were no friends. It was just us all of the time. He monitored everything I did. I tried very hard to please him and took pride in knowing I was a good wife. Maybe not a perfect one, but certainly a good one. Coming from a home where my mother totally catered to my father, I wanted to make my commitment to this marriage a true one. I went along with anything he wanted.

My husband's needs were always first. One thing he really liked was having dinner served the minute he came home from work. So, I'd make sure dinner was on the table hot the minute I heard him pull up in the driveway. It was the same every day, like clockwork. Then one regretful day, he came home from work as usual, no phone call to tell me any change in plans, no indication whatsoever that things needed to be different. I had the table perfectly set with steaming hot food heaped on his plate and ready to eat. The six months we lived with his parents, his mother had taught me to cook and clean and I learned to do both well. This fine day, my husband walked through the back door, walked up to the set table and with one big swoop of his angry hand, knocked everything on that table right onto the floor announcing:

"If I wanted to eat this crap, I would have asked you for it. Now CLEAN IT UP, BITCH!" I was so afraid of him by now, I dared not ask what I'd done to make him so angry. I was willing to do anything to keep him from beating my ass.

The only thing I can remember on the menu that day was the hot loaf of bread I had baked. This comes to my memory because I worked on it several times to make it perfect. My first several attempts had failed. Just couldn't get the yeast thing right. I was producing bricks. But at last, I worked it out, and beautiful, soft, fresh baked bread was on that table!

"OK," I said. "When you're ready to eat, there's more and I'll fix you a new plate." I fearfully stated in a very soft tone while not missing a beat in cleaning the mess as I was told to do.

When I took the broken dishes to the trash out back, I decided to dump the bread loaf in the trash also. Nothing happened to it, but there was no way I wanted him to even know I had sweated over it for him. I've NEVER baked bread again to this very day.

By the time we went to bed that night, he'd made up with me. He apologized as he explained what a bad day he'd had at work, the pressure he was under, and how he wanted to be a good husband to me. Be a good husband to me...be a good husband to me...be a good husband to me. Yeah, I'd heard that line so many times. His pathetic insincere plea was little more than an annoying old broken record.

Bedtime was always apology time, of course, because he wanted to enjoy the pleasures of his manhood. Over and over and over and over. There were times when I was so raw and sore, I would have to sleep with cold rags between my legs to keep the swelling down and sooth the pain of the inflammation. He never made love to me. It was just straight hard sex. I can remember him counting how many times he could come in one night. What was I going to do? I'd become a hopeless, miserable person.

Once, I tried to introduce something new into our sex life (well, his sex life), something I had read in a book or magazine. What did I go and do that for? He rebuffed it, claiming someone must have taught me how to be that vulgar. He insisted he'd have nothing to do with it. The consequences that time? A beating I'll never forget and unfounded accusations of having an affair. I learned my lesson. I never ever tried to suggest he get out of the missionary position again as I laid there feeling like a rape victim with my eyes closed waiting for it to be over. I just wanted him to make love to me once and not make me lay still while he did his duty. I always felt like little more than a human waste bin for his semen.

One day (thank God!), I reached my limits of how much I could take. I decided it was time to stand up for myself or I should say stand up for my children. I'd made a pact with me that if my abusive husband ever hurt the children in any way, I would not hesitate one little moment to leave. I didn't tell him this, but in my heart I knew I was serious. I came to this revelation during one of his many outbursts, when he snatched my daughter (our oldest child) out of my hands and tossed her across the room into her crib so he could beat the crap out of me. I was so afraid he had hurt her, I didn't even feel the blows I was getting for...who knows what? This is when I made a promise never to let anything happen to my babies.

The mailman came to the door one day needing some additional postage for a package we received. Right, the mailman, the milkman, the gardener, pool man, oh well, you know the ol' myth. Well, here I was caught in my own scenario of it; but it was truly a bit different in my case. Being a housewife, you do get to know the people who routinely service your area. I saw the mailman every day and had no reason not to trust him to stand in the door while I went in the other room to get money to pay the balance due for the package. It didn't matter that I was in my neck-to-toe length, thick, quilted robe that zipped from the floor to my chin and hadn't quite started my day. Well, of course, since I was not expecting my husband, he comes home. He finds the door open with the mailman standing in it and completely goes mentally crazy.

I come out and see that there is now an angry, wide-eyed, crazy looking man standing next to the mailman. The look on his face told me I was in deep trouble. I tried to act friendly when I gave the postman the requested money. He thanked me, and then looked at my husband. I know that he knew something was wrong, especially when my husband slammed the door in his face. I wanted to cry out to him, Please come back and rescue me! Hide me in your mailbag, put a stamp on me, and send me anywhere! But I knew that was a bad idea and physically impossible so I tried to act like nothing had happened. I went on about my business, caring for the kids and so forth. It took less than five minutes.

"How long has that been going on? You and that mother f—er are way too friendly for me."

Why did I try to explain? I never managed to say the right thing because there was no right thing to say. He saw things his way and no matter what was said, I was going to be wrong. His anger had to escape and I was always the target no matter what. Only this time, when he knocked me down, I fell hard on top of my toddler. Little fifteen-month-old Kemarah let out a cry that went through me like a knife blade being twisted in my heart. I was really afraid for her. I thought I had broken her tiny bones because she wouldn't stop crying. That was it! No more!

After I calmed her down, I realized she was alright. I put her and our new four-month-old baby boy to bed. While taking a long soothing bath, my mind started putting a plan into motion. By the time I got out of the tub, I knew just what I was going to do.

In the morning, an hour after my husband went to work, not giving him any opportunity to interject his explosive rejection, my nineteen-year-old ass was gone with just the clothes on my back and a baby bag on my shoulders. I never turned around. I only called him once to ask for $20 I needed to buy diapers for the two babies still in them. He refused, saying he didn't want to give me anything—especially money to spend on myself. Fine! I didn't need his little $20, I decided. I managed. And I never asked him for another dime. Ever!

I had gone back home to my parents. Even though he was a monster, he would never disrespect my father by coming to his house to make a scene. About a year later, he called and said I could come and get my things because he gave up the apartment and moved back to his parents' house. I agreed, thinking that since time had passed and he was at his mother's, there would be no episode to worry about. He seemed to be humanly nice about the exchange. It would allow him to see the kids and make peace with me, he convincingly had said. So I returned to a place of horrible and violent memories so I could get my things. A lot of it I had regretted leaving; baby pictures, sentimental items, etc…I thought I could walk on pins and needles for just a few hours without getting punctured.

He traded our car for a motorcycle. His rationale was, No family, no need. It didn't bother me. Made sense, so I didn't question it. Anyway, being very nice, he offered to take me for a ride. I saw no harm, still trusting my instincts and knowing I had to keep peace in order to get my things without any incident. I agreed. He had taught me well, to always agree. So I did.

Just as we were about to ride off, his mother came out of the house. With a motherly concern, she yelled out for me to put the helmet on before taking off. What helmet? I thought. It was then that I turned to see that a helmet was hanging on the back of the bike. So I pulled the helmet on top of my head and fastened it. Great looking out, mom. And God was still looking out for me, too.

Unbeknownst to me, this fool (and I don't call him one without pointing the finger to myself as well; why else would I get on the back of a bike with someone I knew was crazy?) was executing a suicide plan, as he went downhill going what seemed like 100 miles per hour. I yelled out to him to slow down before he caused us to have an accident. He yelled back to me, "I know!" Within moments we crashed smack dab into a car that had stopped for a red light. Knowing this had all been part of his plan, maybe not wanting to, but subconsciously he jumped off the bike before impact. I went flying off the bike. In a slow-motion nightmare, I felt my body slide along the ground, and finally come to a stop when my head hit the ground. The impact had propelled me clear across the street sliding like a bowling ball. My helmet was totaled on one side and the back of my shoulder seriously ripped and bruised. I was hospitalized and lay in a comatose state for three days. He walked away with minor scrapes. Through his mother, God saved my life that day.

When I'd executed my plan to leave him a year earlier, he had executed his plan to kill me. When he came to the hospital, he said only this: "If I can't have you, nobody can have you." Then he walked out. I had no proof he tried to kill me, so I took no action. I didn't see him again for three years. I never got my things.

Now, my children were five and four, and had begun to ask questions about their father. All the other kids had fathers, where was theirs? They wanted to see him. Being adopted and not knowing my birth father, I didn't want to deny them theirs. I always thought the anger he had towards me was just that—anger towards me. Nothing to do with the kids. So, I called him yet again entering into a danger zone. I hesitantly asked him if he wanted to see his kids. He agreed. This time, not only did hell break out, but I felt as if hell had boiled over. In reality that's exactly what happened. Yes, call me stupid, because that's exactly what I was STUPID in all caps.

When you know a bad situation is before your very eyes, that is not the time to shut them and hope what you *know* is there really is not there. Open your eyes as wide as you can and see the danger waiting up ahead. Believe me, caution tape is everywhere. Do not take one step further. Learn from your past. Pitfalls are clearly before you and the best way to escape them is to turn around and go the other way. Please, never ever take risks when it comes to your children! They need you to be strong and make the right decisions for them. It's your responsibility as a parent to protect them.

While he was still living in the downstairs apartment of his parents' house in the View Park area, which is an upscale black neighborhood, my ex-husband began to see his children on a regular schedule. Everything seemed to be going well. I could hardly believe it. I shouldn't have believed it.

I showed up as usual one day to pick the kids up after a visit with their father. When I had called earlier to let his mother know I would be there shortly, I had detected something was wrong. There was just something in her voice, I thought. I passed it off as being paranoid.

When I arrived, I got out of my car, walked up to the front porch of his mother's house hoping to be greeted by my children. To my unexpected surprise, out of nowhere, their dog (a huge German Sheppard) jumped out at me and began to snap at me with every angry tooth reaching out to take in any piece of flesh he could grip. Standing casually beside this viciously attacking hound was my ex-husband, demanding in an absurdly calm voice as he was "sicing" his dog on me, that I get the hell away from him and his children. Once again to the rescue, his mother bolted out of the house wondering what all the commotion was. When the dog lashed out at me, I let out a scream I'm sure the whole neighborhood heard. She ordered him to tie the dog up and let me in. His mother, who had been a nurse, sat me down and questioned me in regards to my little five-year-old daughter having stains and odor in her panties. "It's not normal," she insisted.

I had somewhat detected a slight problem, but I put it off as a result of using the wrong soap in her bath. I thought she was just sensitive to the soap and was hoping a change in bathing habits would clear it up. She was a little girl. What could possibly be wrong? His mother of course mentioned it to my ex before I had arrived, implying sexual abuse. His question to me was, "Who have you had my kids around?" O Mother of GOD!!!! I cried out inside and prayed.

I was in a relationship that my kids were quite comfortable with. They had begun even calling my close friend their play daddy. He was very instrumental in helping me to raise them by being the father image that up to now they hadn't had. Believe me. I gathered my children, headed out of there, and I didn't skip a beat taking my daughter to the doctor.

"Mommy, how come I have to come to the doctor?" Her little soft voice questioned.

Not sure how to explain it to her, I decided to just ask her to trust me and tell me the truth.

"Mommy's going to ask you some questions,

and I need you to tell me the truth. OK?"

At first I didn't think she understood what I was asking her. I assured her everything was going to be all right. Then the doctor came into the room and examined her. While sitting with her waiting for the doctor to reenter the room after his initial examination, I directly asked her once again.

"Sweetheart, I need to know if anyone has ever touched you, ever! I promise, Mommy will not be angry with you. I just need you to tell me the truth. OK?" I spoke in the calmest and most caring tone I could muster.

"OK." Her little five-year-old voice trailed off. Then she decided to be courageous. "Daddy did."

"Daddy?" I questioned again just to get it straight. "What daddy?" My voice sounded puzzled even to my own ears.

"You know. My Daddy," she insisted.

It took all I had to keep my promise to her and stay calm. I needed to know everything and the only way she was going to tell me everything was for me to remain sane.

"Sweetheart, tell me what happened. Please." I added.

"I asked Daddy how the bed got wet and he said the dog jumped in the bed with us and got it all wet." Her attempt at telling the story didn't make sense. But at least I was sure what daddy she was talking about, since my friend didn't have a dog.

I tried again. "Wet the bed?"

"Nooooo. The dog wet the bed and got my clothes and legs wet too. Daddy even wiped it off my privates," she explained.

"Did Daddy hurt you?" I was holding back the angry tears. My heart bleeding with pain, I contained myself for her sake.

"Nooooo......" she replied, shaking her head, convincingly. That was all I got from her. Then, I had to leave the room. I had to get out for just a few minutes to clear my head. I was convinced something happened. I just wasn't sure what that something was.

As soon as the nurse came back in and told me the doctor wanted to talk with me, I asked her to sit with my little girl for just a moment. I went out to get a fresh gulp of air and let me tell you my heart sank as I lost it.

How could I have been so stupid? So in denial of the danger? How could I have let this happen? After all I had gone through, why would I put on blinders, now knowing how unstable this man was? Even today I blame myself for putting my children in harm's way. When you don't completely know what the devil is capable of, you certainly don't subject your innocent children to deal appropriately with someone that has "maniac" written across his forehead and on his chest.

I went back into the doctor's office with my head low, knowing I had let my baby down and knowing I had not kept my promise to myself. Mothers are supposed to protect their children. The most inconceivable thing was yet to come, though.

The doctor came in and we discussed what my little one had just told me. It was then that the doctor threw a blow at me that had such an impact, it literally hit me right in my guts and burst them wide open. I was engulfed in so much pain, I don't know how I managed to walk out of there after he told me what he did.

"Well," he began. "This is serious. There was no penetration, but there had to have been some direct contact somehow. I have to tell you, she has gonorrhea."

"WHAT! OH MY DEAR GOD, NO!" I really needed help with this one. If ever I needed God to hear my prayer, I needed Him to hear me now. Tears rolled down my face faster than I could control them. But I couldn't let my little girl see me cry. After all, I had promised everything would be all right. I didn't want her to feel she had done anything wrong. I stood, turned my back and cleared my face. I told the doctor exactly what she had just told me and wanted to know what to do.

"I will have to make a report to children's services and the health board. So, I need you to write out a statement telling what you know," the doctor informed me in a very clinical manner.

My head was swimming and my heart was pounding. After I did as the doctor asked, he gave me instructions on what to do for my little girl. I assured my daughter while dressing her that everything was going to be all right and she did good to tell me everything. I told her how much I loved her, got the hell out of there, and went straight to the POLICE!

The molester was arrested immediately. When

I went to court, I read the report that confirmed his guilt. Even though he confessed, it was hard to accept that somebody I knew could be so low. But, there it was in writing. To this day, his family doesn't believe he did it. His mother stood by her son. The one thing that made the truth come to light was one line I read in his statement. It was something like, "She woke me up and I told her the dog wet the bed after I realized I must have relieved myself in my sleep."

It made no difference to me that he hadn't penetrated her or was, as he claimed, not conscious of his actions in his sleep (apparently only once). I couldn't help but believe he knew exactly what he was doing. Why would she not have on any underwear under her gown? He claimed that all she had to wear to bed was a gown, because her clothes were being washed. Therefore, he put her to bed without her panties.

Apparently, the sick son of a bitch ejaculated between the legs of a half naked five-year-old child. His own daughter. God help his soul! He got seven years, but was jailed for only a very short time. I'm not sure how long he actually spent in jail, but I know he got out in less than a year. This is when I changed our names and lifestyle in order to keep him from finding us so easily. We never saw or spoke to him again. Today we try not to even give him an ounce of remembrance

Vulnerable Acceptance

or recognition. I only write him in this book for the awareness of those struggling with abuse. I share with you this story to help you understand you have to protect yourselves and your children.

My son was not affected by the ordeal. He knows why he was not allowed to know his father. OH, forgive me…I guess he WAS affected after all. A young boy growing up without his father and knowing why can be psychologically impacted. I've tried to detour the hurt and what's missing by providing him with what I could to give him a healthy start. However, I'm sure he has had to deal with it in his own personal way.

My daughter, at the time, seemed to handle it better than I did. It was likely due to the fact that she really didn't understand what happened to her. I tried taking her to therapy, but after a while, she didn't want to go anymore.

Today, though I know over the years, she has had to deal with the deep haunting memory of the story of what happened to her as a child, and the fact that she grew up not knowing her birth father, she has persevered. She tells me at times that the thought of it gives her an uneasy and dark feeling; but she doesn't allow it to disrupt her. I am so proud to say, she is one of the most beautiful women I know. She is strong and

127

positive and has developed into a loving and nurturing person.

Kemarah, I love you for you, and for forgiving me for not protecting you from such an awful experience in your young life. Thank you for letting me tell your story in order to help others see how very bad and ugly a situation can get before one wakes up. I praise your courage. I am so very proud of you for all of your accomplishments as a highly intelligent woman, an adoring wife, and a loving mother. It's an honor to have you as a daughter, a big sister to your brother, and a younger sister and an aunt to your niece. You are a loyal and gracious friend to all family members and close friends. You are amazing. We are blessed to have you. MOM

CHAPTER 6

Empowering the Good Side

Sometimes it takes a tremendous amount of disappointments to make you wake up and notice that maybe you're going about life the wrong way. Once you discover this realization, it's easier to recognize your need to redirect your path. Actually redirect your mind set, your attitude and your focal point.

The disturbing experience in the previous chapter I just wrote about was by far the worst over anything else I've had to endure in my lifetime. However, I could go on telling you about other deceptive characters I involved myself with over the years, hoping to develop friendships and lasting relationships, in an attempt to find my own self worth. From how a wannabe female singer that—unknown to me—tried to get me involved in a prostitution con game (to no avail); to an involvement with a Bunko artist that almost got me

FROM SEOUL TO SOUL

arrested in one of his hustling schemes. I was way too wet behind the ears to be hanging with this crowd. Man, my mid-twenties were wild times, but I had to learn the hard way and ended up begging God to get me out of a serious mess with a promise that if He would help me, as I was being chased by a police car, I'd never do anything untrustworthy again. I have kept my promise.

Those were the years. Wow. What a rude awakening to a world I was totally unprepared for. Up until that era (my early twenties), I'd led a completely sheltered life. I went from a strict home right into an abusive, controlling marriage and now here I was on my own, to make decisions, fending for myself with two little dependants by my side (my parents were aging and unable to help me with the kids as much as they wanted). Our survival was achieved by my working three jobs and struggling through morning classes trying to finish school.

My kids were with me most of the time, since baby sitters weren't available. They were my little shadows. Many times the kids would quietly sit through my lectures or, when my parents were up to it, they would come to the campus grounds and sit with them on the grass, outside of whatever building my classes were in that day. Because their good behavior was crucial to my being able to go to school and work, they were expected to be quiet most times. People would ask how I got them to sit so still while holding their hands. I didn't know then and I don't really know now. God must have helped me out with that too. They were just well disciplined. Both were excellent children and obeyed me promptly.

My schedule got crazy trying to finish school and work. I worked one job in the afternoon after school at a jewelry distribution center, and one at a night club (where the kids often slept in the manager's office). At two in the morning after the club closed, if we weren't lucky enough to get a ride home, we'd board a bus. (Six months of this and at last I got a little car, a green Pinto.) The third job was playing the piano for a small church on Sundays, which included rehearsal once a week. However, my schedule was always changing as my employers allowed me to put in hours when and where I could. The night club, Disco 9000 on Sunset Boulevard, was where I met many of the characters I thought to be my friends. Most were challenging experiences I outgrew. (Thank God!)

I had now entered a place my parents called "worldly." The people I met and the places I went were so entirely different from anything I'd known my entire life. I was a PK, Preacher's Kid. I'd led a life of going to church almost everyday and being around an older group of staunch Christians and family members. During and after most of the ordeals I went through, I had given up the church and went on my way to live in this world.

These days I found myself partying at every hot disco club in LA. We called it club hopping. I'd managed to meet the president of a limo service that gave me free rides as a business trade for introducing him to some of the celebrities I had also met. The girls would all meet at my house, where a group baby sitter and a limo were waiting. The party was on all night every weekend. Let me tell you, we were truly what they call today "the IT crowd." Unfortunately, you meet a lot of wrong people that, if you are not on top of your game, can influence you and misdirect your purpose in life. This is exactly what happened to me. My trust in others was misguided and led to living recklessly.

The biggest mistake I made was not remembering God made this world I was so clueless about. I should have let him be my guide through it. It was time to wake up and get things in order and get on the right track. Focus, China, focus!! That became my mantra.

Recapping my life, I wanted to ask myself, why on earth did I allow such abusive and negative characters to lead my way? How could I not recognize the signs of confusion? How could I have done things differently to have kept all of those things from happening? I've come to the conclusion, not to ask how or why, just begin to draw from the good things that have happened and learn from the bad. And certainly not to make the same mistakes.

It's simple, if you focus on the positives in your life for all of your life. But it can be a hard thing to do when you feel you've had a rough beginning and you feel all you had was bad. The key is to stop focusing on the downside of your life. Persuade and inspire yourself to think beyond the limits of the past. Empower the good side.

Become who you need to be for you and stop the madness. You've survived the bad experiences, so now it's time to focus on the good ones. Awaken them and start making them part of your existence. It begins with realizing you are not stuck in that old muck, and that there is a way out and it starts with as many good memories as you can bring to mind. Lift yourself up, work on building your confidence, and focus on the brighter side. Yes, it's just that simple. The minute I let go of all the foolishness…WOW! A new world opened up to me. I surrounded myself with positive people and a positive attitude. Even through the hard times, I found myself happy. Then, the miracles started flowing in.

Great things started happening. New alliances, new arenas were always at my reach, but it was I who had chosen to waddle in muck so thick, I felt grounded in it. But it wasn't my foundation; it wasn't what my house was built on. I allowed my mind to take me away to a place I could no longer reside. In truth, it was the good memories that brought me home and into a new light.

One of my very close friends, Travis, told me something one day that hit me like a ton of bricks that weighed me down until the day I made a change. He said something like, "China your life is like a continuing saga of bad luck and there is always something going on with you, girl. When are you going to realize you are a talented person and have some great things going on? You have so much to offer, but it's going to take you to change things and step up to making your life as wonderful as you are."

Travis, thank you for always encouraging me and believing in me when I didn't believe in myself. Thanks for always being on the other end of the phone or across the table from me while I shared my many problems and life's pitfalls. You are the only person that knows just about everything about me. Thanks for holding my secrets. Thanks for taking risks on my behalf. Thanks for being an adopted uncle to my children. You are a true friend. You changed my phone number and address in your book so many times it put a hole on the page. Thank you for that. I know, I still owe you a new book. But seriously, thank you for helping me see my potential and opening up my eyes to change. Thanks for throwing that brick at me!

I will admit, change didn't come easy at first, because I thought change meant starting over. So, I moved and when that didn't work, I moved again, and then moved again and again. I kept saying I was starting over, but actually I was running away from my problems, not embracing what was good.

There was an era when I moved so many times, the number exceeded my age. I think I was always running away because I thought I could leave bad memories behind me; but they would just follow me wherever I went. Truth be told, sometimes I was running from the last month's rent probably sixty days past due. I told myself, I would just start over. I moved so many times, I got really good at it and could pack, move, and unpack in three days. One day for each task. You could come to my house on the fourth day and think I'd been living there for years (not a box in sight).

Even with all that moving, I looked on the bright side and came up smiling. I had to have been a very organized person to have moved so successfully so many times, not to mention strong. I found out how incredibly strong I was. Literally. It's hard to find people to help you move, especially when you move once or twice a year. I'd find help somehow, but once, my family was helping me move my piano into the truck and they almost dropped it. Stevie Wonder was one of my close friends and he had given me that piano as a gift. When I saw it falling, I ran over, got under the piano and basically moved the damn thing myself. I never asked people to help me move without doing as much lifting as they did or sometimes most of it. However, I have to say...

Mike, thanks for all of your help, muscles, and most of all the talks and encouragement!

When I moved from Los Angeles, venturing off to live on the other side of the country, it took me four days to drive a 22-foot truck, pulling my car behind me, alone and fearless, to Florida. The prospect I was expecting didn't pan out for me, so I moved again in another truck, same deal, same way, and ended up in Atlanta. Over the years, I moved via this scenario to New York, back to Atlanta, home again to Los Angeles, on to Denver and finally decided LA was the place I need to be in the end. No place like home.

The city we lived in the longest during that time was Atlanta. I really tried to make it home for me and my children, who were fast approaching their early teens. My son Chino wasn't quite sure he wanted any part of Atlanta then, mostly because he wanted to return to LA and live with Dakota (the father image that helped to raise him like a son). Dakota's home kept my children grounded and gave them an opportunity to go to Lutheran schools throughout their grade school years. He was a Lutheran school teacher. After a lot of drama and struggle to make a decision, I allowed Chino to go back to LA, but not before my little cook almost burned down our apartment. OK, I get it. You really wanted to go back to LA! Oh, just kidding. It really was an accident.

When the smoke alarm went off, my seven-month-pregnant self ran down the stairs, and— through the smoke—discovered the kitchen was on fire. Chino had gone to bed after washing the dishes. He'd forgotten one of the burners was still on as he was trying to melt left over grease used for one of his many meals he prepared for us. (He charged us to eat, I must add. He'd set up a business in my kitchen!)

I was a flight attendant for Eastern Airlines at

the time and while they were having a strike, I was also on maternity leave. Of course I had learned some fire-fighting techniques and was able to put out the fire without any serious damage. It wasn't long after that day that Chino got his wish and returned to LA to go to school. The little happy camper left Kemarah and me in Atlanta to fend for ourselves. And so we did. Chino would later return to Atlanta a year after he graduated from high school to attend Morehouse College. He made Atlanta his home long after I relocated back to Los Angeles years later.

Speaking of pregnant, I had been in a relationship that for the most part had ended. We had planned to marry one day, but the plan just fell through. About two months after we decided to go our separate ways, I found out I was three months pregnant. What was I going to do? First of all, it was too late to do anything, but even if I had a choice, I would never have had an abortion. But I was in a dilemma. I was more worried about what on earth was I going to tell my teens.

It's very hard when you are a single parent to preach to your kids not to end up pregnant or, in my son's case, not to mix himself up with some little fast girl. Let me say this. It was consequently an embarrassing time for me. I was mostly afraid of the reaction I would get from my daughter because I think we are harder on the girls about these things than we are on the boys. Plus, girls mature faster than boys and I really didn't want her to make any mistakes she would later regret. The two of us, like most mother and daughter relationships at that age, were having a hard time anyway. Like many mothers, I really didn't want my daughter to grow up so fast. She was in a hurry to be a woman and I knew she wasn't ready.

Her popularity at school always landed her head of everything. She was named Homecoming Queen in junior high and high school (twice in her junior year and twice in her senior year). As a mother you really are proud, but at the same time afraid. The good side was, both of my teens were very mature about the news of my pregnancy. Neither one judged me. In fact, they welcomed the idea of having a little brother or sister. Kemarah decided to be my Lamaze coach. We took classes and she said she was ready.

December 1, 1990, the day my baby was born, Kemarah was in the delivery room with me holding my hand and helping me along. But as she watched, I felt the tight grip she had on my hand begin to slip. I'm in the middle of pushing out a baby and found myself tightening the grip of my hand trying to hold on to her. I cried out for someone to "catch my baby." The doctor and nurses assured me everything was going well. "Just keep pushing," they insisted.

"No!" I cried. "Catch her, she's falling." Kemarah was slipping from my hand in slow motion to the floor and when everyone realized what was happening, all but the doctor left me and ran over to help her to keep her from hitting her head as she fainted. Class was quite different than real life, with your mother spread out on a table pushing life right out of her. Moments later, the doctor announced, "It's a girl."

My cousin Carole from Atlanta named one of her sons Iman. I thought, Wow, I really like that name for a boy or a girl. So, I knew I was going to use the name Iman for sure. If my baby was a boy I also wanted to use my father's name, Ewing. Iman Ewing was a great name for a boy. But my baby turned out to be a beautiful girl. An unexpected blessing to add to the two blessings I already had.

At first, I tried to create a name for her by combining everybody's names. Kemarah hated it and told me not to use it. "It sounds way too ghetto, Mom," was her official opinion. I had just read the book *Coco* about Gabrielle Chanel and how she built an empire through an amazing struggle. I really was impressed. Not to mention, the Chanel line is one of my favorites in fashion. I had been involved in the fashion industry for many years and I thought, Yes, this will be the perfect name for a girl. Chanel Iman.

I named her Chanel Iman Robinson, giving her my last name because when she was born her father was not at the hospital to sign the papers. In Atlanta, if the mother is unmarried and the father is not present, the hospital insists on giving the baby the mother's last name. That was perfectly fine with me. I wanted her to have a strong name that could carry on my father's legacy anyway (my generation was the last of the Robinsons). Little did I know that thirteen or so years later her name would give way to her own legacy in the fashion world as a rising top model. At least I gave her the perfect name for it! Chanel, you should thank your sister for making me change my mind from the first idea I had for your name, and giving you one so appropriate for you. (No, you don't want to know what it was going to be.)

I have to tell you this story. My three-year relationship with my baby's daddy had finally come to an end, and I decided to move back to LA. Chanel was about four months old and my oldest daughter, Kemarah, and I were traveling through Mississippi. We were tired and traveling with a baby wasn't the same as traveling alone, so we had to stop. While I was looking for a cheap place to stay the night, driving around in a big truck, I accidentally hit an overhead sign at one of the inns we stopped at. I got out to inspect the scene. I looked at the top of the truck, and found that I had put a hole in it. The hotel sign was not damaged, though. I went into the inn to inquire about the price for one night. It was a bit high for us, so we moved on to the next inn down the street. No one said anything to me at all about the sign. After all, it was fine, not dented or anything. Just a big hole in my truck that I knew I would have to deal with once I returned it.

Before we got settled for the night, I climbed up on top of this big ol' truck and taped up the damage, just in case it rained. Everything we owned was inside that 22-foot Ryder truck. I didn't want any problems or anything to crawl into it for that matter. Well, in the middle of the night, we hear a knock at the door. Huddled together in a small room on a small bed, Kemarah and I looked at each other wondering who could be knocking on the door.

"Police. Answer the door ma'am."

When I questioned them what was going on, they asked me if that was my truck. I told them it was, and they promptly began to arrest me on a hit and run charge. As they started to read me my rights, I thought to myself, "What?!" I knew I hadn't hit anyone, but my *rights* were still being recited. What was I going to do way out in the boonies with a teenage daughter and a little baby heading to jail? Leave them alone to fend for themselves? We really were beside ourselves and nearly in tears.

After they read me my rights, they informed me that I had hit a sign. I told them I got out and checked it and nothing was wrong with it. They said the owner took down my license plate number and made a report, so they had to follow up. I had insurance, so everything turned out OK. What a scare for nothing! By morning, we hit the road and never stopped again. I learned on that trip my true endurance. Fear and faith kept me awake and I drove non-stop (only for gas and food) until we reached Los Angeles. Back HOME at last!

Empowering the good side of life takes concentration and stepping back in memories that one tends to take for granted. Every bad experience has lessons to be learned and somehow your strength carries you through. But included in all of that are things that happen in our lives that we perhaps see as ordinary life challenges. Fact is, if you look at it in a different light, the brighter side, you may discover how many blessings shine around you.

Travis was so right. At one point, I had to literally recap my life and realize that as far back as I could remember, I had blocked out the wonderful things that were going on around me. It was so easy to focus on the horrible things that I hadn't allowed the amazing world to emerge to take the lead in my life. I was so worried about being rejected that I didn't see the world had actually embraced me. If I had not let the power of one person distract me for most of my young life, I would have welcomed the challenge to find Yung Sook sooner. Clearly, I was blessed to have had so many people struggle to save my life in the first place and then end up in a loving home where I truly had an amazing childhood.

In spite of my differences with my mom, she gave me so much, because she gave me what she could of herself. My father, the most amazing man I've ever known, was more than anyone could have ever had the pleasure of having in their life. My father adored me and my mother taught me many things that I still use in my life today. Without them I could have ended up who knows where. Instead, I grew up learning to respect and honor a culture that made me proud. I was raised by a family that had many legacies and moments that made me want to shout out to the world, "This is MY family!"

My father was always a positive man and could find good in anything. For example, one Sunday we arrived at church to find the members upset, running up to him saying, "Rev. Robinson, someone broke into the church and stole the organ!" He went inside to evaluate the damage. "Thank God they didn't burn the church down," was all he said. Service was held as usual and he sent up prayers for the thief. No matter what, he always found some way to see a half full glass, never half empty. Even if you dropped it and it shattered into pieces, he'd say "Thank God you didn't cut your foot."

Once I recaptured my life with positive thoughts, I was surprised to find I really didn't miss out on much after all. For me, I was so busy letting that chip ride on my shoulders, it almost detoured me off a cliff. Once I redirected my way, everything fell into place. Everything started to look different. I no longer looked at myself as being different, I looked at myself as being free. Free to explore a world I was afraid of and free to embrace all challenges. I walked into them with confidence and pride. Proud of myself for accepting me.

CHAPTER 7

Closer Than You Think

C aught up in my personal journey and the world that changed for me, I never gave much thought to the question, "Where are the thousands of others that were also rescued like Lee, Yung Sook?" You just kind of think, it's impossible to know about them all, so you move on with no thoughts whatsoever. Or, you stand in fear of stepping into the "It's probably too hard to look into" territory. Funny how we do that with so many things that come to mind. We merely dismiss them only later to find out with a little interest, all things are possible.

Through the perils of time, inevitably we're forced to confront any fears we may have, somehow forcing us to come onto the battle grounds with them, as I well know and have done. If not submerged into my own version of more fears up ahead, I'll welcome a new venture to "Reach Out and Touch," as the famed Diana Ross song goes, to "make this world a better place, if you can, just try." All it takes is effort. Try!

Addressing my own life and coming to terms with the identity crisis I'd allowed myself to get caught into, later discovering the blessings that emerged from all my challenges, It was *all about me*. With very little thought in regards to others in the same light, I clearly had no mental concerns about their lives and what their journey's outcome was or how their roads may have turned. Not to say I didn't care, but one typically never lets what is not in her face merge into her presence. Perhaps it's because one deals with so much already in the daily scheme of things. Even after self-reflecting, however, one realizes, she's not in anything all by herself. The world doesn't just evolve around *you* or just because of *you*. There are others just like *you* out there! Thankfully, there's a natural urge to know who they are.

In the scope of it all, it's that fear of not knowing which complicates and confuses us. It's much easier to dismiss any questionable ideas of "let me look into that" stirring around in your head. I've never been one to ask a lot of questions that don't directly apply to me, so it's hard to envision myself going around a group of strangers hearing my voice asking them to tell me their stories as I dig into their past. However, if I change my thought process just a bit, I could find myself embracing and welcoming the challenge to hear with my heart each and every one of their many experiences. It's not that I don't want to know, it's the asking that seems invading. I've always felt that "If someone wants you to know something, they'll find a way to tell you their business," without having to ask at all, as I have in this book.

In fact, many stories are there. I've even heard a few. There are so many of us! Don't get me wrong, this doesn't separate me from the African American family that I've known. It just adds me to another layer of family acceptance which helps me embrace the once forbidden world. They are me and I am them, this I clearly understand now. We all have been reborn and rooted to the families we now know and love. Stories have walked through my doors out of nowhere bringing my awareness that they do exist.

I was dating someone in my late twenties that told me his ex-wife was half Korean and Black. At first I thought, Sooooo you have a thing for *Blasians*? It was something I'd dealt with many times before. I met a few men that only wanted to go out with me because of their *thing* for Asian-looking women. Oh yes. Exactly! If you're thinking what I'm about to tell you.

There are those out there that will *ONLY* date a race of their choice for *ONLY* one reason: what they feel that race offers them. For *SOME* men that do this type of dating, for example non-Asian men who only date Asian women, they do so because they are stuck in a stereotyped idea of what they think they will get. Some of the narrow minded reasons I was often told by them are that Asian women are submissive, take care of their men, and give good back rubs or better still know how to walk on men's backs. Oh, I kid you not. I have been told that so many times, I know the signs of how to quickly reject these stereotypical, tasteless come-ons. So sad. Believe me, I'd close the door on any suggested dialogue that reveals even a hint that this type of small-minded person is up in my face. When meeting people, if I introduce myself as China then get that "*OOOOhhhhh China Dolllllll!!!!*" reaction, I stop it right there! I don't allow anyone to call me China Doll for that very reason. *Hate it!!*

In the case of the man I was then dating, he assured me it was just a coincidence. To his credit, I must say he is a great guy and was not with me for that reason. As he continued to tell me about his ex-wife, I learned she had come over to America from Korea around the same time I did through the same Holt program. Because he hadn't spoken to her for some time, and didn't want to drudge up old memories, I took it in as "How interesting" and that was the end of it.

One of my mother's good friends had adopted a boy and later a girl. I used to go over to their house and play with them. The little girl was part Mexican and the boy was part Chinese. Of course I didn't know any of this then, but the young boy (older than I was) was the closest person to me that looked like me. It was my one confirmation that black parents sometimes have children with slanted eyes like mine. Much later when I found out the truth, it disappointed my childhood memories of having a lookalike who validated me in my community.

I read in the news that former Pittsburgh Steeler Hines Ward had come forward with his story, which began almost twenty years after I came to America. As stated in articles, his Korean mother was shunned for marrying a black GI in Seoul. His story is similar to mine in that his early beginnings as a child were full of the pain of being cast out in the neighborhood where he grew up because of his Korean and African American mixed blood.

Visiting Korea today as an advocate of change for the acceptance of biracial youth, his vow is to help the many mixed-race children still being mistreated. Creating awareness with his influence as one of the nation's greatest sports heroes, Ward's hope is to make people look differently at mixed-race kids by setting up a foundation for them, according to the article I read. I hope to meet him one day and thank him.

Recently, and I mean within the last few years here in my mid fifties, without searching, I've come to realize I'm closer and have been closer than I think , to lookalikes that have actually traveled on some of the same roads I have. Though their roads have twisted and turned in many different directions, I'm discovering their journeys have crossed my path, finding me longing to know their stories. I understand their struggles and care for them as sisters and brothers from the motherland Korea. So many of the out cast "war babies" literally have been right in my backyard all along.

One day when I walked into a clothing store I operated at the time, my business partner told me a woman had curiously walked into the boutique the day before, apparently wanting nothing. She just looked around but didn't want any help. The woman had been told by a friend of hers to visit the store and when she got there she would know why she was there. She was given no other explanation as to why she should visit, but it clearly wasn't to shop. My business partner then continued to explain how the lady recognized a picture I had of my daughter on one of the counters. The conversation went something like this:

"That model, Chanel Iman, is one of my favorite models. I've been following her since her beginnings.

Her mother is half Korean and black and I am too."

My store partner then told her, "Chanel's mother is one of the boutique's owners and will be in tomorrow."

"Do you know if she is from Seoul and came here through *Holt*?" How ironic. "I didn't know why I was supposed to come here today," the visitor continued, "but now I know and I will be back tomorrow." She thanked my partner and went on her way.

The next day when she walked in....we both knew! It was quite a reunion and let me tell you, we were grinning from ear to ear. It was like looking in the mirror. I hugged her and immediately we became Seoul/soul sisters. I found out she was raised in the Compton area, a community in Los Angeles very close to Watts where I was raised. We knew some of the same people and our first-born children are around the same age. Both girls. Just like that, I had gained a new sister named Kim and a new niece. *WOW*.

Three-year-old Kim, Jung Ja came to America in 1956 (Kim being her last name). Her little heart's desire was to find a family who would show her the love she longed for after living in a foster home facility in Korea, before joining the Holt family of outcast orphans.

Instead, when that day came, her anticipating family took one look at her and their hearts would not open up to the sad little girl. Her skin was too dark, her hair too nappy, and the big unsightly boil on her head made them cruelly call her ugly! Rejecting her, they demanded, "Send her back. She is ugly and not healthy. We don't want this one."

Before Holt could send her back, as God's Grace would have it, a miracle placed her with a family that gratefully added her to a growing bunch, where two other orphans already had been received with open arms. "We'll take her," they said. Within a year or so, yet another boy came to join her family, which would eventually grow to include four orphans. They came from Korea within a year and a half of each other. First, there was a three-year-old son. Then an eight-year-old sister arrived. Kim joined them at age three, and the last to come was another three-year-old boy (none of them are blood related).

As I listened to her story, I remembered wanting sisters and brothers of my own. To me that would have been a dream come true. After hearing Kim's story, I could only say God knows best. OK, maybe I was good being an only child.

Kim's older sister who came before her was told

by her birth mother to go to America in search of a better life. She promised her daughter that she would also come to America and find her so they could be reunited. The mother had been in love with a GI that was deployed in Korea. Out of this relationship came this little girl, and they managed to be a happy family during his stay. But the day came when he went back to America with a promise he'd return for them. When the mother realized he wasn't returning soon enough, she convinced the girl to go on ahead through the program. Korean life would have resulted in brutal treatment of the young girl.

The mother kept waiting for the father to return. He never did. The little girl waited and waited for her birth mother to one day come and get her. She never came until years later, when her daughter was a grown woman in her fifties. This final reunion with her aged mother was distant and unconnected. However, during the many years in waiting, this little girl grew bitter and intolerable. She took out her frustration on her siblings and the anger within her was lashed out on the entire family. The family weakened and as time went on, the home became dysfunctional. The strict parents began to beat the kids to keep them in line. Most of the conflict was because of the older sister, who would scream at the adopted mother. "You're not my mother!" She'd yell as her rebellion and anger grew. Fact is, she never wanted to share a home with other siblings, hated the idea of it, and never shared her personal things.

There was a particularly heartbreaking story Kim told me. One day her sister had a piece of fruit. It was the last piece of fruit in the house, and Kim wanted a bite of it. "You want a bite?" her sister asked. "Yes please!" Kim replied, enthusiastically. The sister then took the fruit and vigorously rubbed it up and down her private area, making sure her body touched it entirely. "Here, now you can take a bite!" When I heard this story, I thought, What anger. What terrible pain, to have known her birth mother and father, been forced to leave them, and finally and tragically lose faith in a mother's promise. What devastating disappointment to endure in such a young life.

Kim's story is quite different than mine, for her parents tried to keep Kim and her siblings connected with their heritage. They would sing Korean songs, eat Korean foods, and even went to a Korean church for a while. In fact, Kim's identity crisis didn't start until after she began high school. That's when the "What are you?" questions began to attack her from the many minds of those who have-to-know-what-you-are in order to fit you into their world.

Like me, for Kim, fitting in was an issue that caused her to make many wrong choices in her life. It took a long time for her to be true to herself. So often she felt alienated by her peers. In time, she realized she didn't have to keep trying so hard. Well into her adulthood, overcoming the desire to fit in didn't come easy and in truth she admits it lingered until 2008 when she came to understand, "God loves me." At last, she'd found acceptance within herself.

In 1983 she joined a Motherland tour to Korea along with thirty-eight other adoptees. Motherland tours is a program that arranges yearly trips to Korea, allowing former adoptees to see where they came from and how the program works. As the tour ends, it's set up to bring more Korean babies to America.

Enjoying the experience, Kim went home satisfied in spite of no records found on her. But the visit was very informative. In an invited gathering, a woman who had once been Kim's foster mother, who kept her before she came to the United States, recognized Kim. She told Kim she remembered how the military police had found her on the streets and brought her to the home. The lady remembered how sickly Kim always was. She told her the man of the house gave her a name because she was nameless when she was brought to the home.

In fact, she had been given several names once in America, including one given to her by the parents that rejected her. So, when she was naturalized as an American citizen, she decided to keep her Korean name, Kim. There she was, on tour at that very facility where she received her name, where now baby shoes blanketed the stairs. On landing after landing hundreds of shoes where children, in care, were waiting to be adopted. The tour gave Kim an assurance of how blessed she was to have been saved.

Months later I was at a play in a small theatre in Los Angeles. One of the young men in the play looked at me several times. Beautiful, tall and talented, his performance was amazing. However, every once in a while I'd spot him glancing over toward me. After the show, all the actors came out to the lobby to meet and greet. He walked over to me and apologized for staring at me. "I'm sorry for staring at you, but I kept looking at you because I thought you were my mom. You look just like her. She doesn't live here and I knew she wasn't coming to the show until tomorrow when she comes to town. I have to show you her picture." He opened his phone. There it was, a picture with such a resemblance to me, I almost thought it was me. There she was. Another lookalike.

He began telling me small parts of her story that sounded oh so familiar. Seoul and Holt connected the dots. We just had to meet. Later he brought her and her husband to my store. Once again, the hugs were on! Another sister and a new nephew that I adore!

Kim, Soon Bok or Soon Bokie as she is called (ONLY by her father; no one else is allowed!) is now known as Margot! She has been Margot since 1958, when at age four and a half she almost missed coming to America because of chickenpox. As the rescue efforts made their rounds again to Korea and back, within six months, now in better health, her papers were in order to come to the United States. Margot's adopted parents, "Amazing people" she calls them, opened their home to four orphans. All the children were about six months apart in age. The first to arrive were a three-year-old boy and four-and-a-half-year-old Margot. Then almost five years later after begging their parents for a new brother and sister, the two became four. They not only got their wish, but were allowed to pick out their very own siblings to join the family! Another girl and boy arrived to make the family complete. Just like my father explained to me, "chosen."

For the many mothers that found it difficult to take care of their little mixed children, foster homes and facilities all over Korea would take them in until they could be placed in the program that would send them to the U.S. and other parts of the world. These foster homes were holding places for hundreds of orphans just waiting to leave Korea.

Margot once knew her mother. One of her brothers was found and brought to a home like Margot (then Kim) by military police. Her other brother was badly abused. Her sister was from a family with blood siblings, but the family was unable to take care of them all, and she was given away. Margot's Korean birth mother knew it was beyond her ability to care for her child. So, she took her to one of these homes. She religiously visited her every day, though, while waiting for another world to open its arms and receive her small child.

When little Kim, Soon Bok's day came to leave, I would imagine that once she was finally gone, her mother had to have truly mixed feelings: tears that she'd never see her baby girl again and gratitude that her child got a chance to go to America. I asked Margot if she ever wanted to find her mother again. Her response was "I feel some things need to be left alone. I feel she should know in her heart, she did the right thing." Yes, she probably did believe in her heart she was giving her child away to a better life.

Who would have known that in the package with a better life of a home, loving parents, siblings, the American dream with endless opportunities also came a world where fitting in at times would be unbearable? The one struggle these little ones were hoping to leave behind. The sense of not belonging. Who would have known the streets were not paved with gold and welcoming mats of pearls like so many believed it would be (like Margot explained was her sister's expectation)? What a disappointment to discover how complicated it turned out for the Korean outcast Amerasian children; to come full of hope to a better America and again be outcast by those they grew to trust and those they wanted so desperately to be like.

We were a different breed altogether, like strange invaders popping up here and there, faces unfamiliar in neighborhoods dealing with their own complexities of acceptance as a black culture. During this time, black mixed children had to be placed in black family homes. White mixed children went to white homes. I've often wondered if the white mixed children suffered the same as we did trying to fit into our African American neighborhoods. I know for me when approached by whites in regard to my nationality, their inquisitive nature has always lacked warmth, yet was infused with wonderment of wanting to know for the purpose of satisfying their curiosity. It's never been mean-spirited. Nor have I felt any sense of mistreatment from whites because of my mix. However, they do a lot of assuming that you are some mysteriously exotic being in some way. It seems to puzzle them and they can't quite figure you out.

But for the African Americans during those years when we came along, being different was intrusive into their world of "I'm Black and Proud." It could have a lot to do with that light skin-dark skin thing that was going on (and still is to a degree). Then to add to the communities' larger struggles with discrimination from white society, here we come with these slanted eyes making things worse as far as taking attention from their plight. Our look just felt out of place in a society trying to find its own place and voice in which to stand. We were the odd ones out and some of them didn't hesitate to let us know all of them didn't have to accept us.

While listening to Margot's story, I was glad to find out it wasn't only me. We all wanted to be accepted by those we most cherished, those who surrounded us. Our black peers. That is why fitting in was *SO* important. I wore an afro as big as I could get my hair to rise up. Margot's hair was finer and she couldn't get her hair to, as we called it, 'fro up. So her mother bought afro wigs for her and her sister. They wore them proudly to prove a point, as I did trying to fit in. Of course, no one was the wiser that they were wearing wigs, but it validated them into the *Sistahood* world to which becoming a member meant at last fitting in. Nothing else could possibly be as important during those days. Called Ching Chong China for so long, I deeply feel the hurt as Margot describes how she and her siblings were called "Black Japs" and "Big lip Japs." Names odiously handed to her in junior high. Having siblings helped her cope with the teasing because they all went through it together. People, by example, teach your children teasing and bullying is so hateful. It alters the lives of those who are targeted by it. To have to endure such treatment is cruel and unnecessary.

Overall, her childhood was good even though there were some family issues, causing her parents to divorce when she was twelve. They were close to her grandparents on her adopted mother's side of the family, as they were very warm and welcoming to the children. Interestingly enough, it was her adopted father that was once in the war and as a GI was aware of the many children left behind. He was the one to suggest they adopt the little ones. However, his parents and family struggled to understand why they would do such a thing as adopting these children.

Like Kim, Margot also went on one of the

Motherland tours that were two weeks long. She stayed at the Holt orphanage and found the experience to be informative and enjoyed it as a trip, but had no yearning to find her birth mother. Margot spent some time in Hawaii and there, blended in with the Hawaiian natives. She found herself realizing that looking like everyone else wasn't what she wanted after all. She has come to a place of understanding that you can't change others, so accepting yourself as special gives you the power to stand tall in your own unique beautiful skin. Eyes and all!

The few examples I just mentioned don't even begin to scratch the surface of the possibilities of the reunions that have happened and those that are ahead. Funny, there's always that familiar refrain of, "I know someone who knows someone who was adopted from Korea during that era." "Hey did you know, one of the Jackson Five, Jackie, was married to Enid, who was a Korean War baby?" Well, I've unleashed the fear to take off wherever it may, which leaves me standing with open arms to find the many that are out there wanting to be heard.

I know these new family bonds are not blood. But who knows? If we were to check into it, we may discover that's possible too. It's not important. What is, however, is the fact that we have found one another.

Each of us has found another soul who understands we are connected through the love of those that rescued us from the hands of thousands who didn't realize how precious God's gifts are.

The victory here is we've all had to learn that self-acceptance is the most powerful healer through all the trials of discriminating discontentment we've had to overcome. From a systematical homogenous era to knowing we are survivors of the fate put on us as an outcast mixed race, we stand strong as a group who can now determine our own fate as we choose.

CHAPTER 8
A Legacy of Pride

One of the best things that ever happened to me was my father. The one thing that I truly should thank God for, if I never thank Him for anything else in my life, is the one thing that kept me grounded even when I was at my worst. My father! As I ponder this thought deep in my soul, both my parents were God-sent, each in their own way. If my father was the gem, my mother certainly helped to make him shine. As they say, Behind every good man there's a good woman. She was his right hand and in his mind always the better half. That says a lot about their relationship and the marriage I so wanted to fashion mine after.

I think that over the years when I look at the disappointments I had in my love life, I have to admit, secretly I'm envious of my mother. She had what every woman dreams about but few ever get to have: a man who loves and adores you just for being you. No expectations, no false hopes, no reason to change you. He only looks upon you as if you are the precious being that you are.

That also says a lot about my father and the kind of man he was. He was a man with dreams that came true, a man that welcomed the world to enter his world. He had a heart full of love for not only my mother, but for me. He adored me and took the time to let me know that every day I had the pleasure of looking up to him so he could smile his love upon my face. I so took him for granted growing up. I wonder sometimes how on earth I missed all of that. My only regret about my parents is that I don't think I ever told them how grateful I am to them for opening up their hearts and giving me a home. I opened my eyes way too late.

My father taught me the lesson of giving every day of his life as I remember him. His giving went far beyond the idea of what giving is generally believed to be about. I'm not talking money or wealth. He wasn't a wealthy man. In fact, as I remember it, we used to say he was somewhat cheap on certain things. He would drive across town to save a dime on a can of practically anything that was on sale. I never understood that. How could he not realize he was wasting more on gas than that dime he was saving? Well, nobody's perfect and I guess it was all about principle.

When it came to giving from the heart to make sure the less fortunate would have a better way, my father was there. You'd find him everywhere there was need—from donating clothes to the homeless on Skid Row after giving one of his messages there to helping a neighborhood mother who needed food to feed her children. Seems like we were always on a mission to rescue, save, or just offer a kind word and—of course—a heartfelt prayer. I grew up in tow while he visited many hospitals and homes of the sick and shut in.

During my father's early teen years, he was determined to work and help out his family. He had only one pair of shoes, and they were so worn that there were holes in his soles. He claimed, like every father, that he literally had to tie the shoes on his feet as he walked miles and miles to get to work. OK, we've heard this story before. What makes this unique was his giving heart that gave with no other reason than to make sure someone else had a better day. "Life without giving is like living without a heart," my father used to preach.

The people who owned the farm he worked on decided to give him a new pair of shoes to make his journey a bit easier to walk each day. My father thanked them and went on his way. When he returned the next day with his old shoes on, they asked him, "Ewing, where are your new shoes?" He simply replied, "I gave them to my brother because he needed them more than I."

As a kid, I had a pair of shoes for church, a pair for school, and a pair to play in. The play time shoes were always an old pair I had worn out. During the summer months, I got a pair of sandals and a pair of soft tennis shoes. I always begged my father for extra pairs of shoes; but we differed on the topic of shoes. Whereas he thought one pair of shoes was enough, I thought you could never have enough shoes. I begged for them as if I was begging for a lifeline. I wanted to have as many as I could get him to buy. Well, he'd recite this story to me and tell me when I buy a new pair of shoes, I should give away an old pair to someone that needs them. Of course, he gave his new shoes away before he even thought to take off his old ones.

I developed a fetish for shoes and today I have so many I can't even count them. I do try and give shoes away because I know my father is looking down and shaking his head. I once worked for an organization called Shoes for Children. I have to say, that experience made me truly understand what my father's point was all about.

Father was born in Ogden, Utah in 1915, to a young former school teacher and a railroad cook. My dad was one of five children—two girls and three boys—during a time when finances were strained. My cousin Deborah recently reminded me, however, that even though they had very little, what was important during their upbringing was the love they had for each other. That love transcended their poverty at the time and it instilled in them the love that they instilled into us.

The former Supervisor of Los Angeles, Kenneth Hahn, was one of my father's dear friends in college. Daddy would tell stories of how "Kenny," as he would call him, supported him through friendship by insisting he be included in everything from sports to campus groups and clubs. During a time when blacks weren't often seen on university campuses, Kenneth Hahn would take a stand and say, "If Ewing is not allowed, I won't participate either." He was instrumental in helping my dad make it through his years in college, as he became the first black to graduate from Pepperdine University in 1943, graduating a year after Hann.

Mother's beginning was as far from my father's beginning as you can get, although they were both from large families. Born in 1915, eight months earlier than my father, mother was a society girl. (She would never have admitted that or told her age for that matter, but I found out through their death certificates.) Her family was from Shreveport, Louisiana. My grandfather, who had died long before I came along, was half French and half black. He was much older than my grandmother, who bore him eight children. The couple and their offspring could pass for white. Their eldest child died as a young girl, but the remaining seven siblings all had enriched lives. With boy names (Lee, Freddie, Dean and Johnnie), my mother and her sisters were beautiful girls and on every eligible man's wish list. They had three brothers to make sure no young man's wish came true.

My grandfather was a leader in his community as a noted professor and well-liked minister. Grandmother was a teacher and seamstress. I remember her wearing the most beautiful suits I had ever seen even until this day. Her things were so perfectly tailored to fit her, one would think she was born with them on. Even in her late seventies and eighties, the age when I knew her, she was always stylish and dressed to perfection. My mother, grandmother, and aunts wore fashion as if they created the word. I can't remember a day that I didn't see them in gorgeous clothing with matching accessories. Hats, gloves, and shoes to die for in colors that made the rainbow look dull. "Put on your best and live your life in style." This is something I tell my youngest daughter today, but when I say it, my vision is clearly on my mother and aunts. However, the point I'm making when I say this to my daughter is to "do your best with class."

My mother's family was well rounded and took pride in being well educated. Their achievements were instrumental in creating historical moments: from music, fashion, and travel, to their contributions in the civil rights movements. Spirituals written by my grandfather still appear in today's hymnals. Songs written and produced by one of my famed cousins Skip Scarborough, who gave me my first music lesson, are sung by a host of famous artists (Earth, Wind & Fire, Aretha Franklin, Anita Baker and so on...).

My Aunt Freddye Henderson, in particular, took the '50s and made the decade her own. Once a professor at Spellman College, she was the first black woman to get her masters at New York University in fashion design and merchandising. In the early part of the '50s, Aunt Freddye was the president of the first organization of black designers known as NAFAD (National Association of Fashion and Accessory Designers). With the help and support of Eleanor Roosevelt, Mary McLeod Bethune and Dr. Dorothy Height of the NCNW (National Council of Negro Women), the organization held the first African American fashion show at the Waldorf Astoria Hotel in New York. They couldn't stay at the Waldorf at this time when segregation was at an all time high, so they stayed at the Theresa Hotel in Harlem.

Now that was the summer of 1953 and the ambassador Henri Bonnet was attending the show with his wife. She was so highly impressed with this group of black designers that she invited them to visit Europe to tour and attend several high fashion shows that included Chanel and Christian Dior in Paris (Hardy Amies/London, Fontana Sisters/Milan). This group of black designers was received and treated so well, my aunt came up with an idea. If blacks knew how well they would be accepted, especially coming from a segregated America, they would be willing to travel abroad. In 1955 she opened the first fully appointed black-owned travel agency in the U.S., in Atlanta, Georgia, offering tours in Africa and other parts of the world. For the first time, many blacks who traveled with her agency experienced and felt a sense of freedom.

Aunt Freddye, with her husband Uncle Jake by her side, arranged travel for some of the most influential people of their time, including Martin Luther King, Jr. In fact, she organized the trip he took to Oslo, Norway where he received the Nobel Peace Prize. Now my gracious and loving aunt has passed on, but Henderson Travel and her legacy live on in Atlanta and in Silver Springs, Maryland.

Aunt Freddye's influence in fashion inspired me to be a designer. I passed my fashion sense on to my youngest daughter, who decided to become a model with a desire to walk the runways around the world. Some fifty years after my aunt took her group, NAFAD, to see the Christian Dior show in Paris, Chanel Iman is one of the few black girls walking in the Dior shows today.

So as you can see, blacks have been supporting and influencing the fashion world for many years. Therefore it's a shame we don't see more people of color in leading roles in today's fashion industry. One would think here in America fifty years after my aunt's contributions, there would be more progress. It would be amazing if we could accelerate that progress when it comes to diversity, by everyone taking part in the demand for change and unity. I'm sure my aunt is looking down and is very proud to see her niece making an impact and representing a new era of black models. I know I'm proud.

I wonder sometimes what kind of family I would have had if my birth mother had made a different choice. If I had been raised in Korea, would America have ever crossed my path? Somehow my imagination of that doesn't give me satisfaction that this amazing family I was so blessed to be in would ever have existed for me. You see, this is why God is in charge. He knows exactly what, when, where and how. I am so grateful He knows all the above and I totally rely on Him to take charge and lead the way.

How do you live up to such glorious legacies like the ones I have in my family? The only thing I can think is, for me to just be the best person and mother I can be. Show my children and grandchildren (adult or not) that they are the most important people in my life and I would do anything to help them or make them happy. I try to mentor them from my own experiences in life and offer them the bases on which my foundation was built. I'd like to think they are proud of me, as I am most proud of them. It is my wish that they see me as a sound and giving mother who is someone they can look up to as being their rock. I know they are mine.

I've been given many gifts. An ear for music, an eye for design, creativity beyond most and, oh, I don't know, you name it and I've tried it one way or another. I tend to be pretty good at most things, though I had never really claimed any of it. My father used to call me "Rosie the Riveter." I could fix or build anything with or without directions. But, somehow I never gave myself enough credit for what I could do. I claim myself as a "Jack of all trades, but master of none." That's me, all right!

Typically, I was in and out of one thing and then another. Daddy taught me to learn many things so I would always have something to fall back on. Truth is, this wasn't good for me because I could always say "Next," if something didn't work out. "Next" was always on the sideline and I could move on to something else. However, through it all, I took pride in being a good mom. A consistent mom. A mom with values and honor. Yes I know I had some weak moments as a young mother, but once I learned about the worst things that could happen, I got my act together and strived to be a better mother to my growing children and granddaughters. I certainly hope they can look at me and carry that legacy with them as they parent their own.

To my friends and family, I hope they see me as a giver. I hope I reflect my father's teaching in that department as part of his legacy. I try to give unconditionally of myself and my time to those who are closest to me. I try to reach out and help anyone who says they need my help. I always make sure everyone is OK. I think it is my destiny to see to it that all is in unison and everything is in order with peace. I was brought into this family for a reason, and I know it is deeper than just my life being saved. Saved for what purpose? I'd like to think I am the tie that binds them all together helping to keep the lives of my loved ones connected to hope.

Dear Cousins, (there are many of you) also to Uncle Herb and Meryl, As my parents, aunts and other uncles have all passed on, I want to say this to you. Thank you for your open arms and most of all your unconditional love. There was never a time when I felt different or unwanted by you at anytime. You have always made me feel special and above all like a valued family member. Candy, Toni, my sisters in arms; and I must include Shirley, Angie and Deborah faithfully by my side over the years. You girls are my soldiers that stood by me as we all grew together. Jake, Ronnie and Herb, my brothers I never had and my strength to which I owe much. Carole, Gaye, Linda and Norma, I've always looked up to you and still do. It's hard to imagine life without any of you and to those I don't mention, you've had an unforgettable impact on me one way or another. You all are invincible and forever loved. I include thanks to the Hills and Jacksons, and to "Auntie-Mamma Lee" and cousins I claimed as my own that always supported my efforts and goals.

We are all here for a purpose, so after you love yourself, reach out and show love to everyone around you. There are just too many people in the world to dislike, so why would anyone want all of that bad karma working inside of them? How much better is it to love and be loved? To share and have things shared with you? To give, because when you give, don't you receive? Absolutely! Let your legacies shine with pride, for no matter what they are, no matter how big or small you think, they have been given to you to pass on.

CHAPTER 9

A Model's Story

We all came to the game to see our little star run up and down the basketball court. Tall and thin, long corn rows swaying with ribbons tied on the ends, the eleven year old stood tall enough to be mistaken as being in the wrong league. Not a chance. She was in fact with her age group and very much a star player. The whole family was there to watch as we all have been at most of her games. She ran up and down the court with her long legs and long outstretched arms waving. She was ready to receive a flying ball at anytime. Our screams echoed through the gym. She caught the ball just in time and shot it right into the awaiting basket. Score! The piercing sound of sneakers screeching across the floor moved fast to the opponent's side of the court.

The teams set up once again. It was impressive to see her play with one of the best players on the court, who was the smallest of the bunch. The tiny player stole the ball from the other team, weaved in and out of the scattered players, all much taller than she. She spotted Chanel, who was hard to miss, then strategically dribbled the ball close enough to send it flying into the air as Chanel rushed under their basket, received it, and dunked it for yet another score.

As we sat on the sideline, most often on the gym floor of Culver City Middle School (Culver City, CA), our discussion was mostly about what an amazing future she had and how it was going to be the beginning of a college career we were glad to get ready for. Scholarships, college basketball, on to pro teams and then who knows, endorsements, etc. We went on and on about the possibilities of a great career in sports. On the ride home after the game there was always excitement. Congratulating her, we were so confident about her future as a basketball player. We'd assure her of how much talent she had and how—with a little more passion on her part—she could be another Lisa Leslie of the Los Angeles Sparks. Beautiful, talented, and the focus of many endorsements.

"I don't want to play basketball. I want to model." She'd insist.

"But if you play basketball, you could go anywhere you want to with that. First college, then be on a pro team. From there you could get endorsements and that will give you the in on a modeling career if you still want that. The opportunities are endless." I repeated myself…I don't know how many times. I may as well have been preaching to the basketball tucked under her arm, because I certainly wasn't getting through to the player.

Truth is, Chanel never had a passion for basketball. She liked to play because her friends were on the team and she wanted to do what they were doing. It was only a form of socializing for her. Over and over, since she was a very small child, she said she wanted to model. I'm not quite sure when it started or why, but as far back as I can remember her little voice, she has said, "I want to model." I heard her, but I guess I didn't listen. Actually when she was a toddler, I used to flip through fashion magazines with Chanel to teach her colors and see if she could recognize alphabet letters and numbers. We'd turn the pages calling out lady, man, child, mommy, daddy and models. Perhaps that's when her little mind decided she liked the models and wanted to be one.

Over her young years, she developed a passion for the idea of becoming a model, so much so that everyone knew that's what she really wanted. If you asked her what she was going to be when she grew up, her answer was always "I want to be a model." Never once did she say, "I want to be a basketball player."

There was a time she wanted to be a cheerleader. When she got the chance to be one and even be on the drill team, that dream passed. I think I thought the modeling thing would pass too.

In grade school she wrote a commencement speech that won her a sought after spot in front of a podium at her sixth-grade graduation. I knew then, as she effortlessly gave that speech in front of the entire school and families, her determination would get her whatever she wanted. Two years later, she won yet another chance to give another commencement speech to her eighth-grade graduating class. From there, there was no stopping her.

As a parent, when you see your child as having a talent, you try to lead them along those roads that will help them to achieve reasonable goals. Goals you see as reachable, especially when you see them as having a gift. That doesn't always mean their path is down the road you see them on. In my case, I certainly was planning my child's future on the wrong map. I had to come to terms with Chanel embarking on her own road with her own passions. Because she'd played football, ran track, and was now playing basketball I was sure this was her calling. She'd taken drama in middle school, but that was short lived. I just knew she was bound to be an athlete. After all, her father was a pro basketball player once and is now a basketball coach at a university. (At 6'7", he is definitely where Chanel gets her height.) What a good position to be in: great genes and a connection. I tried everything to get her interested in the game.

Mel, a very close friend, was in cahoots with me in proving to her how good she was. One summer, when Chanel was about eleven or twelve, he was taking his son (around ten at the time) to UCLA basketball camp. It was a camp for over 300 boys. He paid for Chanel to go to the camp even though she was the only girl. At the end of the summer, the camp was giving out trophies. Chanel received two: one for "Outstanding Courage" (which they created just for her) because she was the only girl; and the other for "Most Valuable Player" in her division.

Mel and I were sure that would be enough to convince her of how much talent she had as a player. We couldn't have been more wrong. She did well at camp because she always had a competitive edge. The boys were just a challenge to her to prove she was as good as they were. It wasn't about the game at all or her future on the court. In the end, all she talked about was becoming a model. "See Uncle Mel, I told you guys," she now tells us. Ultimately, my persuasion had no validity up against her passion and convinced me of the seriousness of her goal. The pressures on my part ended without regret and only a slight disappointment trailed to see such talent go to waste. In the end the most sustainable feat is the love to support your child's heartfelt interest.

On December 1, 2003, Chanel turned thirteen. By January 2004 she was signed with Ford Models in Los Angeles.

New Year's Day, 2004. Family and friends were over to our house for dinner. Tita and Chanel had been talking for a while about the possibilities of her modeling. Tita once had modeled and knew about open call day at a list of agencies. She and Chanel came into the kitchen and as nicely as she could, Chanel—with a big grin on her face—asked if I would take her to look into modeling. When I hesitated to answer, Chanel said her Aunt Tita could take her to the open calls and get her started. Tita backed her up by assuring me, "Chanel is now 5'9 and the time is right because the agencies are looking for her size, age, and height." There was a young teen black girl about Chanel's age making fashion news during her rise in a modeling career. I thought "so young," but agencies were looking for girls that fit a certain category (young black teen girl with curly hair), so the timing was right.

A year earlier, Kemarah and I attended a talent search meeting with Chanel. Many parents had brought their children because some scout had given cards out at a mall to kids they thought would benefit in their agenda to make money. Chanel had begged us to go, convinced the man who gave her the card would give her the opportunity to be a model and be in commercials. I don't know why I tried to overlook her persistence in becoming a model, when she was always the Little Princess type. In spite of playing all types of sports, she always made it known she was a pretty girl first. Halloween was the for sure sign that this was the direction she wanted to go. Pretty dresses, fancy hair and make-up with every costume. Dress-up parties were her favorite events, where she and her friends could prance around like little models with faces painted like Jezebel. While I was busy yelling out "go to the back yard, practice your dribble, and shoot some baskets," I'd find her in the mirror creating some new hair-do or trying on my clothes and shoes.

I told Chanel if she wanted to really do this, she would have to prepare herself so that if it happened, she would be ready. We practiced walking and posing. There is a big mirrored wall in our foyer at home that we made into a mock runway. We walked and walked as if we were in a real show. We practiced turns and poses. I told her to have a special contact with the audience that was all her own to make them remember her. I think that is when she came up with her signature wink. I went out and got several magazines. I laid them on her desk in her room and told her to study the poses and expressions of the models on each page as if it was homework. I told her that when she was finished, to come and show me she was ready. And so she did.

Unfortunately, the scout was not legit. People, those of you who are trying to get your children into the industry, remember this: If they ask you for money, you are not in the right place. This casting of wannabe agents tried to manipulate us parents, as our children tugged our arms with pleas, while the wool was being pulled over our eyes. I wrote out a check for $700, handed it to the man, came to my senses at the last minute, asked for my check back and got out of there as fast as I could.

We went home and Chanel was so disappointed and mad at me, I think she thought I didn't believe in her. That wasn't true at all, but I just knew something wasn't right. I tried to explain that to her but to no avail. At that point she started to really rebel against playing basketball. I guess if she wasn't going to get what she wanted from me, she wasn't going to give me what I wanted from her.

After finding out just how manipulative the modeling scouts' approach was, I had reservations about the idea of her starting so early and thought I would do some more research on how to legitimately get started in this industry. However, I had definitely decided not to rush into anything. I knew one day I would have to address the passion Chanel had in becoming a model, but I really wanted her to finish school or at least be in her senior year in high school. I thought she had to develop a little more, both intellectually and physically. My final decision was to wait and try later when she was older.

To my surprise, I gave in to Chanel and Tita's begging that day, telling Tita (and feeling somewhat frustrated at their pressuring me), "OK, then you take her." And so she did. I knew she wasn't going to write a check for $700 so there wasn't anything to lose. The day she took her, I had a flight to work. When I landed and checked into my hotel, the phone was ringing off the hook. Four different agencies, four different ideas why they wanted her, four different people selling me on the reasons why I should choose them to represent my daughter. I couldn't make a decision right then and there, so I told each I had to get home and talk it over with Tita and my daughters Chanel and Kemarah (we call her Asia).

Tita, in case we haven't told you enough times, thank you for knowing where to go and the willingness to take her in the first place. We are forever grateful.

Tita, by the way, wanted to manage Chanel. We found out models don't really need managers like actresses, though. As Chanel's mother, I began traveling on the road with my child, signing contracts, organizing her travels and working with her agency. I started managing her mainly due to the fact that she was a minor when this all started. As her mother, I also managed her personal assets and business affairs as well as oversaw her best interest. Plus, Tita had a young son to look after and as it turned out would not have been available for such a busy travel schedule. However, we certainly value her initiative and insight in getting Chanel into this industry. In fact, Chanel calls her Aunt Tita. Today, as an adult, Chanel is self managed and I now act as her assistant, helping her in any way necessary.

Getting back to that day, in the end we all decided on Ford because we had heard of and respected their history and appreciated their sincere proposal. They were the only agency that offered a contract for a year. That meant we wouldn't be stuck if we didn't like their representation. The other agencies wanted at least a two-year contract. It was the best move and we remained with Ford for six years. I will always give credit to them for putting Chanel Iman on the map as a name in fashion to recognize. Guess what? They never asked me for one single dime to get her started. After Ford's ownership and management changed we thought it best that Chanel move on. She later signed with Supreme for a very short time and is now with IMG, one of the largest modeling agencies in the world.

She began her career as just Chanel. I insisted on them using her first and middle names, Chanel Iman, and I'm glad I made a big deal about it because the name caught on and made her a name to remember. Ford strategized her career from day one, making sure she was never moving too fast or lacking in any way as she grew in an industry that has many ups and downs. Models come and models go. For Chanel, we curled her hair (it wasn't a natural curl) and she worked from the day we signed and continues to work on an A-list scale, defining her as one of the top-paid models of her time. Each year as she grew, her career developed and molded to heights we had never dreamed of. The rest is history and we don't have to curl her hair anymore.

By the way, that wink she came up with captured the attention of the one and only editor-in-chief of *American Vogue*, Anna Wintour, while walking on the runway wearing designer Phillip Lim. Less than six months after she winked at the famed editor, Chanel ended up on the cover of *American Vogue* as one of ten "Next Top Models," all personally selected by Mrs. Wintour. Chanel was the youngest at sixteen and the only minority. She was the third African American to grace the cover, following behind Beverly Johnson and Tyra Banks (though there have been other blacks not from America, like Naomi Campbell).

So as you can see, wrong as I was, I had to redirect my vision and join Chanel in hers. The minute I found out how serious this industry was about my little girl, I got right on top of making changes and sacrifices. It's what we had to do to keep up with the demand of her career in order to make it work. The first two years was all about getting to know what a model's world entails. Teen magazines, department store catalogues, and some commercials was the beginning of it all. Kohl's, Macys, Bratz Dolls, and Target. But by the second year, bigger things started to happen and she was maturing right before my very eyes. One day she was a little basketball player and the next she was a young lady with major goals finding her own way in fashion while walking in runway shows of the top designers of the world.

New decisions with every level were imperative

to Chanel's success. Chanel's school and my job were blockages that could have made the difference between "in" or "out." Of course school was important and my job was needed to survive. Though she was making money, in the first few years of a career like this one, most of the money you make goes back into the development of the career. So, in fact, most of the money she made was not enough to live on. Not to mention, it was *her* money and we wanted to put as much of it away as possible (in my mind this could be college money for the future). How were we going to keep up with the demand and hold on to what was important to us, which was education, survival, and maintaining our home?

The decision was made in 2005 when Ford invited Chanel to participate in Ford's 2006 Supermodel of the World search held in New York City. In this prestigious competition, she would be running up against fifty models from around the world and Chanel was going to represent the United States. I threw a big "Champaign and Cider" send off party for her, inviting friends, family, Ford models, *Teen* magazine editors, and their staff. We all toasted her after Mel Foster (my good friend and spiritual advisor) blessed her with a prayer for God to oversee her career and keep her safe during her travels. We all wanted to send her off protected and loved. "In all thy ways acknowledge

Him and He will direct thy path." (Prov. 3:6)

Mel, Thank you for always being there for me and for your support, prayers and valuable advice over the years. You are my dear friend and confidant. I don't need to be reminded about the love that surrounds me anymore, but please keep praying for us.

At the competition she came in third place and won a $50,000 contract. Coming in third never slowed her down. Actually her career turned out better than the girl that won. Chanel's career boomed into orbit and designers around the world wanted her in their lineup as a must-have "new face" model. The decision was to either give it all we had or step back and have a catalogue career. Good, but not good enough for a rising star. So we soared ahead.

I had been working on remodeling my house. It was half done when all of this started happening, but I dropped the project, took out a second loan on my home, enrolled Chanel in an online school, and took a leave from work. Soon we found our lives completely changed. We woke up in New York, Milan, Paris and London on a whirlwind fashion world tour that blew our minds season after season.

Each day on the tour, the now fifteen-year-old, 5'10" Chanel, with me in tow, worked from early morning until late evening. Every chance we got, in between shows and down time, we studied and did school work. She was a good student and I did everything I could to help her through the stress and keep up with her demanding schedule. As a team, we managed to get it all done, completing school and maintaining her job. It was a God-send the day United Airlines offered 200 flight attendants an early out in 2008. I had been saying all along if they would give me my free flight benefits, I would leave. And so it was, that's when they offered the plan. I took the early retirement offer and was relieved that I could now manage Chanel's career full time without worrying about my schedule with the airlines.

I missed my personal life, but I knew life was really good for me without it. I am sometimes in awe at how amazing things turned out for us. I often turn to Chanel and thank her for taking me on this journey with her. As a flight attendant, I have seen the world. But to tell the truth, I have never seen it like this. When I was in the fashion industry, it wasn't on this level and the scene is totally different on this side of the fence. With Chanel's career, I have been to places I never thought of going. The places I've been before somehow look different. The experience certainly is one of a kind. From New York, London, Milan and Paris to Iceland,

Switzerland, Spain, different parts of Africa and my favorite experience, Seoul, Korea. Even the amazing locations in the States are overwhelming. From Palm Beach and Miami, Florida, Hawaii, New Orleans to the white sands of New Mexico just north of El Paso. Locations for photo shoots that take your breath away and that keep your mouth wide open saying, WOW!

I was a little nobody designer, but I now have met the biggest and top designers of the world. I've had the pleasure of meeting the best editors, photographers, casting directors, stylists, and hair and make-up artists in the business. So many new faces on our agenda every week and all so very welcoming and genuinely fond of Chanel. It makes a mama proud! Oh, I knew I'd get my personal life back one day, but nothing could compare with the enjoyment I was now having, watching my baby grow into a fabulous woman. Not so much because she is a successful model, but because she claimed it and worked harder than anyone I know to make it happen.

I've always told her, if she discovered she didn't like modeling anymore, she could stop at any time. Thing is, there were times when she was sick, suffered a broken foot, a burned leg (that got infected after she dropped a curling iron on it), contracted food poisoning and became dehydrated. But this arduous kid applied mind over matter and was so professional about her work, you would never have known any of this was going on as she insisted on walking down the runway without one indication of how ill she really was.

When she broke her foot, Oscar de La Renta, Jason Wu and Michael Kors all arranged for her to have one shoe her size and the other shoe two sizes larger to accommodate her broken foot so she could walk in their shows. We kept her foot on ice right up to show time. Against doctor's orders, she put that size 7 ½ shoe on one foot and the size 9 ½ on the other and walked on those runway as if not a pain in the least was going through her throbbing foot. We left New York and traveled with that broken foot the entire season through Milan and Paris. Thankfully it healed properly.

Once, designer Erin Fetherston had a chair sitting backstage at the start of her lineup for a very sick Chanel to sit until it was her turn to go out onto the catwalk. When it was her turn, Chanel got up, walked the runway with perfect timing, and upon her return backstage literally fainted into my arms. Needless to say, she didn't make the finale. Erin was understanding and wanted to let Chanel out of the show as sick as she was, but Chanel had insisted she was not going to let her friend down at the last minute.

Chanel missed her personal life as well. She had to sacrifice the experiences that high school offers: teachers (not an internet screen), classmates, friends, and social functions like the prom. But how many teenagers can say that on prom night they were walking on a red carpet at one of fashion's most prominent galas, the Met Ball? In a dress designed just for her as his entry by top designer Phillip Lim, who escorted her to the event, no less. It made missing the prom not so bad.

I think what she missed most was her family and friends when she was away on tour. Truth be told she really missed soul food. This girl loves to eat, especially soul food and sweets. Her thin body had yet to catch up with her height, and gave no indication as to how much she eats. I've read some really mean things on the internet about how thin she is and how she needs to grab a hamburger. Well for those stupid idiots (just to shut you up), she loves to eat at In-N-Out Burgers. She orders a double burger with cheese, a single burger with cheese, fries, a chocolate shake and a lemonade all at once. Before we can get out of the parking lot good, it's almost all gone. Most times she eats three meals a day. If not, she's munching on something all day long. With a high metabolism, I just don't know where it goes. What's important is that Chanel is, overall, healthy and strong.

What people don't understand is the majority of these girls are very young and their bodies just haven't had a chance to mature yet. Because of their height, they look extremely thin. Yes, there are eating disorders that happen among models, but usually it's those models that have been in the business a long time and are trying to maintain that young appearance they once had. Backstage at most of the shows, I'm a witness to the fact that these models eat. The minute the food is laid out, it's gone. They are constantly munching on something.

Usually, the problem is that there is not much time between shows to grab a bite and when the models arrive from show to show, make-up artists and hair dressers are pulling at them saying there is not enough time for them to eat. Most girls didn't have someone like me to make sure no one takes that opportunity from them. I'd walk in with Chanel, she'd be grabbed by someone that immediately put her in a make-up chair, and I'd head to the food table to make her a plate so she could eat while they worked on her.

As we are mother and daughter, I'd be lying to say we never have our spats. During these times, a teen girl and her mother will always think differently. What's harder is a teen with her own career, money, goals and interests. Let's not mention the boys. But, for whatever reason, we got through it and all our spats were short lived. We'd try to come to an agreement and move on. There is always a bigger picture to deal with so even now we both agree we are on the same page, maybe each looking at it differently and coming up with a different interpretation. When it comes to what is real, we both read between the lines and the fine print and get the point.

With all of the hard work—and believe me it is hard work—there are times when we get frustrated. It even gets insane sometimes to the point that we are almost pulling out our hair. Of course, there is always that small group of people that doesn't want you to succeed. Don't get quite why, but they do exist. Many times they're against you for no other reason than they read your name and have to give their opinion as to why they don't like it. I want to ask them, "What awful name do you have and what have you done with it?" Mostly I stay quiet, letting it roll off like water on wax paper. I've always said to Chanel if 90% of the people are saying positive things about you, the 10% that are negative have no voice.

That's when we both have to exercise the "Power of One" to overcome any obstacles that try to block our way with negative karma or input. "Stay focused," I preach. Then we visualize the big picture so we can bring it on home. I say to that small group, "This is bigger than you and bigger than your imagination of it. I wish you the best, and—like it or not—we're doing ours. Oh, we don't need your approval and in case you haven't recognized, our blessings come from a higher power."

With two big brothers (one is her father's son) and a big sister, Chanel is the baby and they all love and support her with a vengeance. Her two nieces, Sanai and Dylan, look up to her as she has vowed to always look out for them. Though her father always lived in another city and on the road as a coach all of her childhood life, he and his wife are very proud of Chanel and try staying connected as often as possible. Chanel's closeness to her family is an indication of why she misses home so much. I know for a fact, she draws strength from knowing how much we love her and that is the reason she tries so hard to be her best. Not only for herself, but for her family. I am most proud that she never forgets where she comes from or that God is always by her side. She was once asked by a backstage reporter, "What, if any, ritual do you have before you go down the runway?" Her response was merely, "I pray."

Chanel once had a fear of flying. As a young

kid she never had a problem with it. After all, she grew up a flight attendant's child. At work we called these kids "airline babies." She was a "United Kid," but as she got older this fear of flying showed up out of nowhere. I'd tell her to pray a "Peace be Still" prayer. "For when Jesus was out on a boat with his disciples, a great windstorm arose, and the waves beat into the boat. The disciples were sore afraid. They woke Jesus crying in fear, He arose, rebuked the wind and said to the sea, 'Peace be still!!' and the wind ceased and there was a great calm..... He then said to his disciples, 'Why are you so fearful? How is it that you have no faith?'" (Mark 4:37–40)

During turbulence, this prayer always works for me and for her. The sky outside the plane calms and even if the turbulence doesn't subside, God calms her nerves and through faith, she knows everything is going to be all right. Even in this rocky business of the fashion industry, when things get rough, I remind her to think and pray, "Peace be still."

From 2003 to 2013 and ongoing, Chanel has thrived in the fashion world. Walking the runways of Marc Jacobs, Proenza Schouler, Derek Lam and Anna Sui she debuted her strut. Then it was on to Milan and Paris, completing her first season with sixty shows that included Valentino, Dolce and Gabbana,

Dior, Alexander McQueen, Jean Paul Gaultier and most of fashion's high profile designers. Each year she continued to be placed on the must-have "A" model list. She was the first black in five years to walk Gucci. From there, it was Versace. Chanel is a Vogue model where she first appeared on the cover in May 2007 as one of Anna Wintour's selection of ten girls to be "The World's Next Top Models" photographed by the notorious photographer Steven Meisel. Endless shows, campaigns, and covers fill her portfolio with fashion's most impressive credits. It is a list long enough to say this girl really knew what she wanted to do and nothing was going to get in her way of proving she was born to be free to do exactly what she wanted. To be a model. A top model. A Supermodel, that is!

In 2010 Chanel received her wings as one of Victoria's Secret Angels. DKNY fragrance, Target, Amazon, Microsoft and Intel are just a few advertisers using her name to sell products. Bookings continue in 2013 to vault from cosmetic lines to Sports Illustrated. She remains on the invite lists of the most famous and receives invitations to be an honored guest at numerous galas that include the White House. She has been invited by Michelle Obama several times to the White House and other events. Chanel is respected for her work on Obama's 2012 reelection campaign, during which she worked side by side with noted top celebrities.

In her first two years on high fashion's catwalks, Chanel was one of the very few black models seen in the shows. Often, she was the only one. Each time she was asked about being the one and only black girl in a lineup, in a chided manner she'd let the press know, she wished there was more diversity hoping to never hear designers again say "we already have one black girl we don't need you any more". History in this industry has been fickle (mostly hesitant) when it comes to color. Black models have had an up and down presence as if it was a fad. It's sad that designers, as creative as they are, aren't creative enough to see that color will only enhance their lineups and not take from them. One gets tired of hearing this or that designer is not using a black girl this season as if it is in bad taste. "We used a black girl last season, we don't have to use one now." Once, Chanel heard a stylist yelling out to her dresser, "We're not putting that dress on a black girl. Take it off of her."

Chanel's voice, as an advocate for diversity, has been clear and strong on the so often controversial subject. Today, where you do see many more black girls along with other minorities, we are proud to feel she has had some impact on this situation by letting her voice be heard. Press and internet forums sometimes try to create rivalry among the black models by making statements like, "There's only room for one black girl, this one is in and that one is out." They try to stress which one is booking more shows over the other. They want them to compete. Competition is fierce among all models. Everyone is trying to book jobs. Although it is implied the black girls hate each other, many are surprised when they find out the girls are friends or friendly. They support each other and wish each other well. They are not rivals. Come on people. They are sisters all working towards the same cause and goals.

It's not just the designers who are to blame for the lack of diversity. Agencies, casting directors, stylists and art directors and including advertisers make up a powerful group that could change things but won't. Everyone's waiting for somebody else to make a move. The first ten to twenty pages of any magazine present the major problem, with advertisers using only the common choices that don't include models of color. So those pages are as colorless as they can get, and it will stay that way if we don't step up. Of course, there are few and rare exceptions, but normally if they decide to use color, the black model is replaced by a high-profile black celebrity. The black model works just as hard as her peers. Actually, she works harder because she has to see twice as many designers to get fewer shows than her nonblack counterparts. And let's not talk about major campaigns. The model of color is still waiting for her day to regularly shine on just one of those glossy pages.

On the topic of diversity on the runway, in a *People Magazine* interview with Modelinia in 2009 during People's 25th Anniversary shoot with Chanel Iman and Iman; Iman is quoted as saying "It's amazing at this age 2009 almost 2010, with Obama in presidency that we should even be talking about this. It's kinda weak! But you do the best that you can and here really just be true to yourself." Chanel adds, "You gotta stay positive and secure with yourself and do you."

For now, that's just the way it is and as we wait for a change to come around we will just have to keep representing the best we can. To the few that are visible, I say, Strut your stuff and remember you are making a difference. Maybe soon the decision makers like those who hold on to that old line of reasoning "color is distracting," will discover color can brighten up their day.

Everything happens for a reason. I do believe some of the things I went through as a young adult prepared me for these days so that I would know how to endure the pressures of this industry and help Chanel through it all. I have no idea what lies ahead for Chanel or for me for that matter, but what I know for sure is this. She is my daughter, I am her mother who is very proud of her, and no matter where either of us ends up, this has been an incredible life. We will never forget this as being a gift from God.

In 2008 we found out just how much God's hand had been in making this all happen and how things go full circle when you leave everything up to Him to fight your battles and give you just what you need even when you don't realize you need it. Early on I fought Chanel on the idea of becoming a model. It was her modeling career that not only made her dream come true, but allowed me to have one of the most unexpected experiences of my life. "A mother's journey and a daughter's dream" that merged together giving way to an experience that brought me back once again to my roots in a style I would have never thought possible. And so the story continues.......

CHAPTER 10
Seoul's Black Beauty

"Heaven came down and glory filled my soul." I felt like singing that song when I was surprised one day by a phone call that told me my prayers had been answered! My hopes had always been to one day have the opportunity to return to Korea in living color, and let me tell you, living color it was. Even if it had been in black and white, it would have been spectacular. The most amazing thing I could ever have imagined in my wildest dreams happened and completed my long awaited ending to a once painful struggle and beginning. Nothing like closure with a peaceful ending. An ending with fireworks. An ending that was a beginning of a new enlightenment.

Lying in bed one August morning in 2008, contemplating my day, I was trying to decide if I wanted to eat breakfast out or just have cereal. It was all I had in the house. Chanel's then agent called from Ford Models. Paulo was on the phone overcome with joy. "It's out, my love, it's out. The cover, it's beautiful, go get it!" He exclaimed in his strong Brazilian accent. "You'll love!" He insisted.

"What cover, Paulo?" By now Chanel had been modeling for four years, and her modeling career was steadily climbing. She had already been on several covers and I don't know how I forgot, but I guess I was still in awe and disbelief about the possibility of such an amazing outcome. Then immediately I remembered, "*Vogue Korea*?"

"Yes, my love. It's beautiful. You may have a hard time finding it, but try my love, you'll be so happy." He insisted.

"Thank you, sweetheart, thank you. I know just where to go! I love you!" I said almost breathlessly and hung up the phone. I quickly got dressed and went straight to Korea Town near downtown Los Angeles. Near Western and Olympic, I parked my car. In Los Angeles we have cultural areas. Olvera Street, China Town, Korea Town, etc. When you drive through one of these particular areas, there are signs indicating you have just entered a certain cultural neighborhood. Here I was in Korea Town where signs were posted to let me know I was in fact in the right place. It took a few stops in and out of several stores before at last I saw it on the shelf. I don't think anyone will ever understand the height of my emotions and exactly what seeing that cover for the first time meant to me. What stirred inside of me is unexplainable.

Almost exactly fifty years ago, I left Korea as an ostracized orphan because of the black American blood that ran through my veins and now here on the cover of *Vogue Korea* was my very own daughter, Chanel Iman. Her beautiful, slim form was standing over the heading, "Black Beauties." I was beside myself! What an amazing flip of fate. I thought, "As the world turns, so does the heart."

Several months earlier, when Paulo called to tell Chanel and me we were going to Seoul for a photo shoot and cover story, we both hit the ceiling. Our joy level was so high, you could almost see the fireworks sparkling as we danced and celebrated the whole night. She was happy for the opportunity, but I know she was mostly happy she would be able to take me back to Korea in style. Again, a mother's journey and a daughter's dream was about to come together as one finale orchestrated by God.

Style it was, and we were welcomed! *Vogue Korea* rolled out the red carpet! Everything was so amazing. The best hotel, limo service, and a welcoming crew that gave us carte blanche. We had several camera crews following us around the week we were there and two top photographers competing for the cover. Both photo opportunities were so amazing, that both were included in the issue along with Chanel's Seoul story about her trip to Korea and my return as an orphan. We toured around Seoul, being wined and dined to our heart's content. It was absolutely the most gratifying trip ever! Not because of all the hype (although that was awesome), but because of the way we were received.

The ignorance of prejudices involves us in unnecessary pain and experiences no one should ever feel. The heartache of its existence is so real. It stunts our growth and can undermine our ability to proceed into a future of unity. So for me, this whole experience united me with a new day, knowing prejudices of the past had evolved into acceptance of the future generation. Even in Europe, where the fashion industry still has its stigmas on change, I feel they are at a breaking point to take their vision one step closer and broaden their perspective on color. America, as diverse as it is, has had it's moments that made you wonder why we are all in denial of how bad things have been for minorities. However, I have faith that we can come together on the idea that we are all beautiful and, make no mistake about it, can grace the pages of any magazine. We've already shown we are willing to take this idea of equality as high as you can get, all the way to the President's seat of the United States of America. Halleluiah!

Shortly after Chanel's *Vogue Korea* cover came out, I was reading some of the feedback about the issue and came across a blog or some other social media forum where they were discussing Chanel being on the cover. Mostly it was positive. As usual, there were those two or three that were not so. Everyone is entitled to their opinions, for I value mine. As I read on, I came across a young Korean girl that stated she was a fan of Chanel's and how excited she was to see her on one of her favorite magazines. Then she added, her grandmother was appalled at seeing a black girl on the cover of *Vogue Korea*. People like that are to blame for children being ostracized fifty years earlier before being rescued from the unkind hands of those who didn't value human life. After fifty years, there are still haters that will never change. I'm so grateful each day that fewer and fewer of them exist. Sad how they are stuck in their own mess.

The first photo shoot went fabulously smooth. Chanel shot the editorial with Hyoni, another Ford's Supermodel of the World winner (2008) who represented Korea and is full Korean blood. Also working with them were two Korean male models that were absolutely gorgeous. The clothes were beautiful and each set was elegant, full of color and styled with a theme "Trend Atelier" by photographer Hyea W. Kang. The photographer kept telling us how happy she was with the shoot and showed us most of the images on her computer. Yes, I agreed they were some of my favorite pictures. Everyone was wonderful and acted as if we were honored guests. I did feel honored and was treated with complete respect. They were fascinated with my story and one of the young ladies promised to help me with the research on my book. After the shoot the photographer and her assistant took us to a traditional Korean dinner.

The second photo shoot was amazing, as well, and Chanel gave the photographer OH Joong Seok everything he was expecting from her. It was a black and white story titled "Black Break." He told her he was one of her biggest fans. She entertained OH Joong Seok and his staff by jumping, twisting and striking every pose she could think of as the camera clicked, clicked, clicked, clicked, and clicked steadily capturing her every move. You could hear the photographer yelling "Great! Perfect! Yeah, yeah, yeah!" The staff all watched as if she was a performer. To them she was and after the shoot, every one of them took turns taking pictures and getting her autograph.

During our stay, *Vogue Korea* took us on a tour throughout the city. We visited many tourist hot spots. One of the most impressive was the Deoksugung Palace (one of five palaces), a residence once built for a prince. They took us for a traditional dinner where the crew gave us gifts as a tradition. Then the next day we found ourselves shopping at popular city walks along the stone covered streets. It rained and the crew gave us clear umbrellas as if to say, "Keep shopping, we'll protect you." Chanel and Hyoni tried on traditional Korean garb called *hanbok* just like the one I was given the first time I visited Seoul. While we were shopping in the village, we went into one of the boutiques and the sales girls went wild. They knew who Chanel was and with a camera crew following her, it was obvious something was up. You would have thought Michael Jackson was in the house. The girls were all over her with real tears running down their cheeks and high pitched screams squealing out her name. Chanel looked at me with an "OMG, what do I do?" expression. She handled it. I'm sure they weren't expecting a supermodel to walk into their store and make their day.

We did have some personal time alone to go exploring on our own and both Chanel and I had a great time getting to know the city. We were very excited the whole time we were in Seoul. People we passed in the street, though they stared at us, made us feel welcome and at home. Mostly they stared because Chanel is so tall and thin, towering over me as her short and squatty opposite. But we make a good team and have lots of fun.

This trip was certainly unforgettable and the memories will always be among my fondest. Never knowing my birth parents, my mother in particular, I felt a real connection to her during this trip even if we never got to meet. It's not likely and I'm not sure I really want to at this point, but I've found peace in knowing I can walk the streets of Korea and have warm smiles welcome my presence as I pass. And for those stuck in the old world of racial purity I have to thank you also, because without you and your solution to your perceived "worst nightmare," I would not have been part of the most amazing family that loved me unconditionally.

CHAPTER 11

A New Soul

I n this century, only a decade or so away from when I completed my journey, I am inspired by crossroads that take me even further than I could have ever imagined. Crossroads where I've found strength, courage, and valor. What I was ever seeking, to belong and have an identity by common standards, has forced me to turn the page and discover I am surrounded by an insurmountable amount of blessings that exceeds the fear of not fitting in. It has proved to me I don't have to prove myself at all.

The world as I have known it all of my life is so different than through those slanted eyes I was so badly teased about as a child. I proudly wear them, seeing through them true value. Now when I look in the mirror, I barely recognize myself. No, the Barbie doll still is not standing there. I visualize a more amazing dream. Yet, like Barbie I stand tall, my bosom rises high with pride. Not because of the size of my girls, but because of what beats beneath the little sisters. Ken for me may show up by the time you finish reading this book. Who knows? If not, though, I am quite content standing alone.

Soul is not a test of how black you are or how much rhythm you have. It's not your color or your swag. I am bound to soul because I have a connection with myself, my inner being that tells me everything within this body is full of grace and satisfied. What I share within myself to others, determined to commit my love for you and—most of all—me is solid. Soul is the essence of what bonds me to the beliefs I am engaged with, the faith I trust, and the spirit to which I rise. Soul is the inspiration I gain from those I am most inspired by. My soul doesn't falter by things that don't work for me or by those that unkindly disapprove, but perseveres steadily in tune with the tempo I set for myself.

When I was a child, my father baptized me in the Pacific Ocean. Every year we had our annual picnic at one of our local beaches. The beach picnic party was a celebration to those who wanted to get baptized. The church bus was always packed and everyone wanted to come and see the many children and adults in white robes as the ministers dunked them into the salty water. When they emerged from the ocean, they were welcomed by cheering witnesses singing, "Wade In the Water" as they themselves waded in the water along the edge of the shore. Each cleared the water from their eyes, being reborn into this world a new person. "Born again," as the minister preaches.

This Pacific Ocean where I was baptized is the same Pacific Ocean I crossed to find myself among the pages in an orphan book. So I truly feel I am a new person and my soul has been reborn. Not to take away from that born again feeling you get when you are baptized, because being born again in Christ is the most fulfilling life line one could ever own. Baptism is an example of how I deeply feel. It's like I've been reborn again. My soul that is. I now know this new soul has given me purpose and completion.

As I deal with the prejudices of today, though my heart is saddened by what still exists, my soul rejoices for how far we have come as a nation and how much stronger love is than hate. Most prejudices are merely ignorance and misunderstanding of the unknown. My prayer for today is that we will all really try harder to take diversity as a personal goal, and have a desire to see it live. We must have the tenacity to work hard to educate as many people as we can, especially our children, to see every person as precious. The difference in our cultures and skin tones should have no bearing on our position to be accepted or not or our ability to excel or not. You are you and I am me, but we are all human beings. My prayer is for us to walk together hand in hand, soul by soul. Any day, any time, any place.

In 2009, we all had the pleasure of seeing the nation's first black president sworn in, an event wrought with new ideas and a hope of change. This was history made possible by the civil rights leaders of our time and others who struggled for change that came before him. When Barack Obama was reelected in 2012 by the people for a second term, we punctuated the idea that we have evolved. This is a new day and a man who is a living testament to diversity is now ranked as one of the leaders of our world. Deny it no more. For those who fight against this inevitable future, do some soul searching and step into this century with the rest of the world. Old ways and old ideas have crippled us far too long. It's time for a healing. What is needed for us to survive are strong, positive visions that make us understand unity is in our willingness to change and come up with creative solutions that are sound. We must start with a mindset to see the future with all people in it, each doing their part as human beings. The sooner we band together the sooner we will heal.

If you look to the right or you look to the left and you don't like what you see in your neighbor, go to a mirror and look straight ahead. If you think everything in the reflection is perfect and better than any other then there's your problem. Try to envision your hate or judgmental ways then ask yourself why it is in you. Stand there and focus on yourself. Then do something about that person. Maybe you will find peace if you work on what you really see in that mirror. Perhaps you will look again and notice that the right and the left are not as bad as you think once you recognize your own faults. If you become a better person in your heart, your neighbors won't bother you as much and you'll become a happier person for you yourself to look at.

Rome wasn't built in a day. Even God took seven days to set things up for us. There's no doubt it takes time to readjust one's thinking to develop new ways to capture the best out of life. Every day, through technology, advertising, education and most of all through our hearts, life changes and we find ourselves looking at new ideas that erect from our very own needs. What are those needs? What are yours? Everyone is different, yet our common grounds are exactly the same: air, food, a place to live and the will to do so. Let's take it just a little further than that and include love. For with love comes respect, honor, and consideration. One step further and add peace. With peace we are connected to forgiveness, happiness, and unity. So as we inch up, step by step to new horizons, let's remember to embrace our thoughts on the bigger picture and understand, we are all looking for pretty much the same things out of life and no matter which path you travel, meet your new soul along the way.

Postscript

I'm online one day and discover an entire Korean and black community, linked together through social media. They have outings and events bringing this huge *KB* family together (KBC – Korean and Black Club). The blogs and online connections are endless. I'm hoping this book will be yet another tool that links those who want to tell their stories. I'm expecting to hear from so many more. Perhaps *From Seoul to Soul* will find its way to a continuation. Book II, Part II.

Ms. China's
From Seoul To Soul
Photo Gallery

ung W. Robinson 14/2/57

CHILD REPORT

NAME: Lee Yung Sook # 336 HO   GENERAL HEALTH: Fair

BIRTHDATE: Nov. 25, 1955   SKIN TEST: Neg.

ADMITTED: Nov. 15, 1957   X RAY: OK

BROUGHT BY: Orph, Supt.   BLOOD: Neg.

SEX: Female   HAIR: Dark Brown, Sl Curley

RACE: Negro Korean   *Very Light*   EYES: Brown

PERSONALITY: _____   BUILD: Very Thin
Friendly or shy, noisy or quiet,
alert or dull, active or listless,   BEHAVIOR:
affectionate or withdrawn.   Comparison with age group: Younger
                                    Than birthdate
Manner of mixing with other   Does he adjust quickly: No
Children: Doesn't

ADJUSTMENTS:

Would you suggest this child be place in a home
as an only child or should there be brothers and sisters? Only much older
                                          sisters or brothers
Older or younger parents? Younger

SPECIAL REMARKS: This is a nice little colored girl, right now she is
very thin and malnurished, but has gained some. I am sure she
would be happy and loveable if she was well, but now has been in an
orphanage so long, all she can do is cry and eat. She is very tiny
and dainty, and I am sure the birthdate is wrong, as she only has
6 teeth.   *Molly Holt*

336

My Child Report that states I was a malnourished little colored
girl, listless and withdrawn.

(**Left**) My Korean passport picture (Lee, Yung Sook) Dated January 6, 1958. I arrived in the US March 27, 1958. (**Right**) Kindergarten picture 4 or 5 years old.

My first pictures with my Adopted African American Mother
and Father (early 1958).

(**Left**) Happy with my Mother and Father (late 1959)..(**Right**)
Holding my African American Doll with Blonde hair (late 1959).

Happy at home (1960)

With family and neighborhood friends
(**Left**) Cousins. (**Center**) Church friends on Easter. (**Right**)
Dressed like twins with my cousin Candy and Lil Susie from the
corner store.

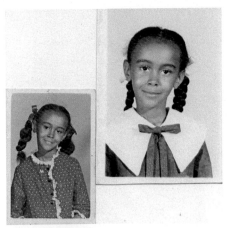

My cousin Candy with her beautiful heart shape face(I invited
her to come to my school).

Candy and me standing
with our mothers and
grandmother 1966/67

Mother's class in 1954 at 109th Street School four years before
she stopped teaching. Impeccably dressed as always.

Father's class in 1954 at Grape Street Elementary (Watts) where he taught for over 30 years.

Mother and her sisters:
(**Top**) Mother and two of her sisters. Mom, Auntie Johnnie and Aunt Freddye. (**Left**) Dressed in high fashion, Auntie Johnnie, Aunt Freddye & Mother. (**Top Right**) Styling in hats, gloves and coats, Auntie Johnnie & Mother. (**Bottom Right)** Mother styling from head to toe with gloves, bag and the pose.

My Aunt Freddye and Uncle Jake (The Henderson's) on a tour bus in Hong Kong

My handsome father the first Black to Graduate from Pepperdine University in Los Angeles. 1943

The Rev. Robinson Speaking at an event with College Friend
Supervisor of Los Angeles Kenneth Hann

My High School Graduation picture. Proving my sistahood with
a big afro on top of my head 1973, Morningside High School.

Returning to Seoul 1997

(**Top Left**) Kemarah & Tita boarding the bus in Seoul that took us to Holt International. (**Top Right**) Me standing in front of the Holt Children's Services building. (**Center Left**) In the records office at Holt International where I found Young Sook Lee (Me) among the record books. (**Center Right**) With the lady and man who first took care of me when my birth mother left me. Now Kindergarten and school directors Mr. & Mrs. Kim, Young-ul. (**Bottom Left and Right**) Molly Holt took me to a Korean dinner.

Me, Kemarah and Tita holding orphan children at the home of Molly Holt.

Shopping in Seoul with Kemarah and Tita

Stopped on the street by young people who thought
Kemarah and Tita were models

Chanel Iman on the cover of Vogue Korea. September
Issue 2008, standing over the heading "Black Beauties." This
is when I knew I had the ending to my book. A complete
transformation than when I left 50 years before in 1958 as an
outcast colored orphan.

Back to Korea with Chanel Iman
Back to Seoul with Chanel 2008. Chanel and Hyoni trying on
traditional Korean dress (Hanbok) and learning about the
culture.

Back to Korea with Chanel Iman
Out touring the city with the crew, Chanel, and Hyoni..

Traditional gift giving from Vogue Korean crew member